MW01234454

LOTUS® 1-2-3®
—— RELEASE 5 ——
FOR WINDOWS™

by: maranGraphics' Development Group

IDG
BOOKS

IDG Books Worldwide, Inc.
An International Data Group Company

Foster City, California ✦ Indianapolis, Indiana ✦ Boston, Massachusetts

Lotus® 1-2-3® Release 5 for Windows™ Visual PocketGuide

Published by
IDG Books Worldwide, Inc.
An International Data Group Company
919 E. Hillsdale Blvd., Suite 400
Foster City, CA 94404
(415) 655-3000

Copyright© 1994 by maranGraphics Inc.
5755 Coopers Avenue
Mississauga, Ontario, Canada
L4Z 1R9

Screen shots [©1994] Lotus Development
Corporation. Used with permission of
Lotus Development Corporation.

Library of Congress Catalog Card No.: 94-73678

ISBN: 1-56884-671-1

Printed in the United States of America

10 9 8 7 6 5 4 3 2 1

Distributed in the United States by IDG Books Worldwide, Inc.

Distributed by Computer and Technical Books in Miami, Florida, for South America and the Caribbean; by Longman Singapore in Singapore, Malaysia, Thailand, and Korea; by Toppan Co. Ltd. in Japan; by IDG Communications HK in Hong Kong; by WoodsLane Pty. Ltd. in Australia and New Zealand; and by Transworld Publishers Ltd. in the U.K. and Europe.

For general information on IDG Books in the U.S., including information on discounts and premiums, contact IDG Books at 800-762-2974 or 317-895-5200.

For U.S. Corporate Sales and quantity discounts, contact maranGraphics at 800-469-6616, ext. 206.

For information on international sales of IDG Books, contact Helen Saraceni at 415-655-3021, Fax Number 415-655-3295.

For information on translations, contact Marc Jeffrey Mikulich, Director of Rights and Licensing, at IDG Books Worldwide. Fax Number 415-655-3295.

For sales inquiries and special prices for bulk quantities, write to the address above or call IDG Books Worldwide at 415-655-3000.

For information on using IDG Books in the classroom, or ordering examination copies, contact Jim Kelly at 800-434-2086.

Trademark Acknowledgments

maranGraphics Inc. has attempted to include trademark information for products, services and companies referred to in this guide. Although maranGraphics Inc. has made reasonable efforts in gathering this information, it cannot guarantee its accuracy.

Lotus, 1-2-3 and SmartIcons are registered trademarks and SmartMaster is a trademark of Lotus Development Corporation.

MS, MS-DOS and Microsoft Mouse are registered trademarks and Windows is a trademark of Microsoft Corporation.

Lotus Map Viewer Version 1.0 © Copyright 1994, Lotus Development Corporation. All rights reserved.

Geographical and demographic data. © Copyright 1994, Strategic Mapping, Inc. All rights reserved.

The animated characters are the copyright of maranGraphics, Inc.

U.S. Corporate Sales	U.S. Trade Sales
Contact maranGraphics at (800) 469-6616, ext. 206 or Fax (905) 890-9434.	Contact IDG Books at (800) 434-3422 or (415) 655-3000.

About IDG Books Worldwide

Welcome to the world of IDG Books Worldwide.

IDG Books Worldwide, Inc., is a subsidiary of International Data Group, the world's largest publisher of business and computer-related information and the leading global provider of information services on information technology. IDG was founded more than 25 years ago and now employs more than 5,700 people worldwide. IDG publishes more than 200 computer publications in 63 countries (see listing below). Forty million people read one or more IDG publications each month.

Launched in 1990, IDG Books is today the fastest-growing publisher of computer and business books in the United States. We are proud to have received 3 awards from the Computer Press Association in recognition of editorial excellence, and our best-selling ...For Dummies series has more than 10 million copies in print with translations in more than 20 languages. IDG Books, through a recent joint venture with IDG's Hi-Tech Beijing, became the first U.S. publisher to publish a computer book in the People's Republic of China. In record time, IDG Books has become the first choice for millions of readers around the world who want to learn how to better manage their businesses.

Our mission is simple: Every IDG book is designed to bring extra value and skill-building instructions to the reader. Our books are written by experts who understand and care about our readers. The knowledge base of our editorial staff comes from years of experience in publishing, education, and journalism — experience which we use to produce books for the '90s. In short, we care about books, so we attract the best people. We devote special attention to details such as audience, interior design, use of icons, and illustrations. And because we use an efficient process of authoring, editing, and desktop publishing our books electronically, we can spend more time ensuring superior content and spend less time on the technicalities of making books.

You can count on our commitment to deliver high-quality books at competitive prices on topics customers want to read about. At IDG, we value quality, and we have been delivering quality for more than 25 years. You'll find no better book on a subject than an IDG book.

John Kilcullen
President and CEO
IDG Books Worldwide, Inc.

IDG Books Worldwide, Inc., is a subsidiary of International Data Group. The officers are Patrick J. McGovern, Founder and Board Chairman; Walter Boyd, President. International Data Group's publications include: ARGENTINA'S Computerworld Argentina, Infoworld Argentina; AUSTRALIA'S Computerworld Australia, Australian PC World, Australian Macworld, Network World, Mobile Business Australia, Reseller, IDG Sources; AUSTRIA'S Computerwelt Oesterreich, PC Test; BRAZIL'S Computerworld, Gamepro, Game Power, Mundo IBM, Mundo Unix, PC World, Super Game; BELGIUM'S Data News (CW) BULGARIA'S Computerworld Bulgaria, Ediworld, PC & Mac World Bulgaria, Network World Bulgaria; CANADA'S CIO Canada, Computerworld Canada, Graduate Computerworld, InfoCanada, Network World Canada; CHILE'S Computerworld Chile, Informatica; COLOMBIA'S Computerworld Colombia, PC World; CZECH REPUBLIC'S Computerworld, Elektronika, PC World; DENMARK'S Communications World, Computerworld Danmark, Macintosh Produktkatalog, Macworld Danmark, PC World Danmark, PC World Produktguide, Tech World, Windows World; ECUADOR'S PC World Ecuador; EGYPT'S Computerworld (CW) Middle East, PC World Middle East; FINLAND'S MikroPC, Tietoviikko, Tietoverkko; FRANCE'S Distributique, GOLDEN MAC, InfoPC, Languages & Systems, Le Guide du Monde Informatique, Le Monde Informatique, Telecoms & Reseaux; GERMANY'S Computerwoche, Computerwoche Focus, Computerwoche Extra, Computerwoche Karriere, Information Management, Macwelt, Netzwelt, PC Welt, PC Woche, Publish, Unit; GREECE'S Infoworld, PC Games; HUNGARY'S Computerworld SZT, PC World; HONG KONG'S Computerworld Hong Kong, PC World Hong Kong; INDIA'S Computers & Communications; IRELAND'S ComputerScope; ISRAEL'S Computerworld Israel, PC World Israel; ITALY'S Computerworld Italia, Lotus Magazine, Macworld Italia, Networking Italia, PC Shopping, PC World Italia; JAPAN'S Computerworld Today, Information Systems World, Macworld Japan, Nikkei Personal Computing, SunWorld Japan, Windows World; KENYA'S East African Computer News; KOREA'S Computerworld Korea, Macworld Korea, PC World Korea; MEXICO'S Compu Edicion, Compu Manufactura, Computacion/Punto de Venta, Computerworld Mexico, MacWorld, Mundo Unix, PC World, Windows; THE NETHERLANDS' Computer! Totaal, Computable (CW), LAN Magazine, MacWorld, Total "Windows"; NEW ZEALAND'S Computer Listings, Computerworld New Zealand, New Zealand PC World, Network World; NIGERIA'S PC World Africa; NORWAY'S Computerworld Norge, C/World, Lotusworld Norge, Macworld Norge, Networld, PC World Ekspress, PC World Norge, PC World's Produktguide, Publish& Multimedia World, Student Data, Unix World, Windowsworld; IDG Direct Response; PAKISTAN'S PC World Pakistan, PANAMA'S PC World Panama; PERU'S Computerworld Peru, PC World; PEOPLE'S REPUBLIC OF CHINA'S China Computerworld, China Infoworld, Electronics Today/Multimedia World, Electronics International, Electronic Product World, China Network World, PC and Communications Magazine, PC World China, Software World Magazine, Telecom Product World; IDG HIGH TECH BEIJING'S New Product World; IDG SHENZHEN'S Computer News Digest; PHILIPPINES' Computerworld Philippines, PC Digest (PCW); POLAND'S Computerworld Poland, PC World/Komputer; PORTUGAL'S Cerebro/PC World, Correio Informatico/Computerworld, Informatica & Comunicacoes Catalogo, MacIn, Nacional de Produtos; ROMANIA'S Computerworld, PC World; RUSSIA'S Computerworld-Moscow, Mir - PC, Sety; SINGAPORE'S Computerworld Southeast Asia, PC World Singapore; SLOVENIA'S Monitor Magazine; SOUTH AFRICA'S Computer Mail (CIO),Computing S.A.,Network World S.A., Software World; SPAIN'S Advanced Systems, Amiga World, Computerworld Espana, Communicaciones World, Macworld Espana, NeXTWORLD, Super Juegos Magazine (GamePro), PC World Espana, Publish; SWEDEN'S Attack, ComputerSweden, Corporate Computing, Natverk & Kommunikation, Macworld, Mikrodatorn, PC World, Publishing & Design (CAP), Datalngenjoren, Maxi Data,Windows World; SWITZERLAND'S Computerworld Schweiz, Macworld Schweiz, PC Tip; TAIWAN'S Computerworld Taiwan, PC World Taiwan; THAILAND'S Thai Computerworld; TURKEY'S Computerworld Monitor, Macworld Turkiye, PC World Turkiye; UKRAINE'S Computerworld; UNITED KINGDOM'S Computing /Computerworld, Connexion/Network World, Lotus Magazine, Macworld, Open Computing/Sunworld; UNITED STATES' Advanced Systems, AmigaWorld, Cable in the Classroom, CD Review, CIO, Computerworld, Digital Video, DOS Resource Guide, Electronic Entertainment Magazine, Federal Computer Week, Federal Integrator, GamePro, IDG Books, Infoworld, Infoworld Direct, Laser Event, Macworld, Multimedia World, Network World, PC Letter, PC World, PlayRight, Power PC World, Publish, SWATPro, Video Event; VENEZUELA'S Computerworld Venezuela, PC World; VIETNAM'S PC World Vietnam

Acknowledgments

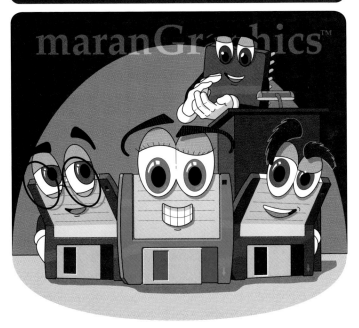

Thanks to Marc LeBlanc of Lotus Development Corporation for his support and consultation.

Special thanks to Wendi B. Ewbank for her patience, insight and humor throughout the project.

Thanks to Saverio C. Tropiano for his assistance and expert advice.

Thanks to the dedicated staff of maranGraphics including, David de Haas, Lisa Dickie, Judy Maran, Maxine Maran, Robert Maran, Sherry Maran, Suzanna Pereira, Tamara Poliquin, Dave Ross, Christie Van Duin, Carol Walthers and Kelleigh Wing.

Finally, to Richard Maran who originated the easy-to-use graphic format of this guide. Thank you for your inspiration and guidance.

Credits

Author & Architect:
Ruth Maran

Technical Consultant:
Wendi Blouin Ewbank

Copy Developer:
Kelleigh Wing

Layout Artist:
Christie Van Duin

Illustrator:
Dave Ross

Assistant Illustrator:
David de Haas

Editors:
Lisa Dickie
Judy Maran
Kelleigh Wing

Post Production:
David McKenna
Kris Gurn
Robert Maran

TABLE OF CONTENTS

Getting Started

Introduction 2
Using the Mouse 6
Start 1-2-3 10
Worksheet Basics 14
The Current Cell 16
Enter Data 18
Enter Data
  Automatically 22
Select Cells 26
Select Commands 30
Move Through a
  Worksheet 38
Getting Help 42

Save And Open Your Files

Drives 46
Directories 48
Save a File 50
Save a File
  to a Diskette 54
Exit 1-2-3 58
Open a File 60

Edit Your Worksheets

Edit Data in a Cell 66
Delete Data 70
Undo Last Change 72
Move Data 74
Copy Data 78
Check Spelling 82

Using Formulas And Functions

Formulas 88
Enter a Formula 92
Automatic
 Recalculation 94
Functions...................96
Enter a Function..........100
Add Numbers 106
Errors in Formulas........108
Copy Formulas...........110

Working With Rows And Columns

Insert a Row..............118
Insert a Column 120
Delete a Row 122
Delete a Column........124
Change Column
 Width.....................126
Change Row
 Height 130

Format Your Worksheets

Change Appearance
 of Numbers 134
Change Number of
 Decimal Places..........136
Bold, Italic and
 Underline 138
Align Data................140
Change Fonts.............142
Center Data Across
 Columns..................152
Add Borders 156
Style Data
 Automatically 162

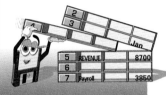

TABLE OF CONTENTS

Print Your Worksheets

Preview a
Worksheet 166

Print a Worksheet........172

Add a Page Break 174

Change Page
Orientation 178

Change Margins 180

Change Printed
Data Size 184

Change Your Screen Display

Zoom In or Out 188

Display Different
SmartIcons 190

Using Multiple Worksheets

Insert a Worksheet 192

Switch Between
Worksheets 194

Name a
Worksheet 196

View Multiple
Worksheets 198

Copy or Move
Data Between
Worksheets 202

Using Multiple Files

Create a
New File 206
Switch Between
Files 210
Close a File 212

Charting Data

Create a Chart 214
Move a Chart 218
Size a Chart 220
Change Chart Titles 222
Change Chart Type 226
Print a Chart 230
Create a Map 234

INTRODUCTION

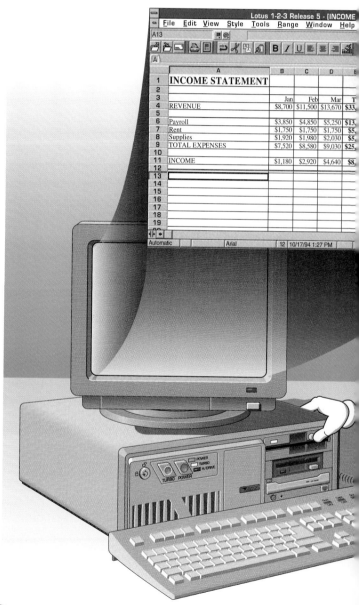

Lotus® 1-2-3®
for Windows™ is
a spreadsheet program
that will help you manage
and analyze your
data.

INTRODUCTION

This is what you can create with Lotus 1-2-3 for Windows.

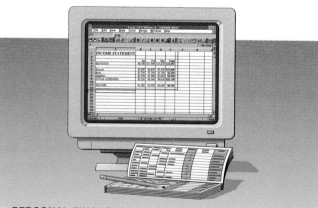

PERSONAL FINANCES

1-2-3 helps you keep track of your mortgage, balance your checkbook, create a personal budget, compare investments and prepare your taxes.

FINANCIAL REPORTS

Businesses of all sizes use spreadsheets to analyze
financial information. 1-2-3's formatting and charting
features help you present your results in professional
looking documents.

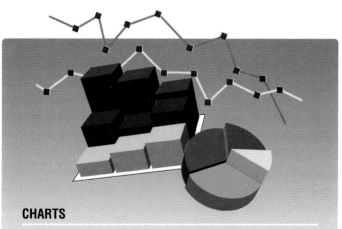

CHARTS

1-2-3 makes it easy to create charts from your
spreadsheet data. Charts let you visually illustrate
the relationship between different items.

The mouse is a hand-held device that lets you quickly select commands and perform tasks.

USING THE MOUSE

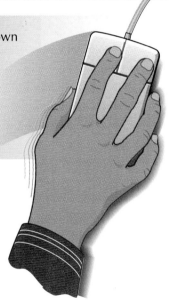

◆ Hold the mouse as shown in the diagram. Use your thumb and two rightmost fingers to guide the mouse while your two remaining fingers press the mouse buttons.

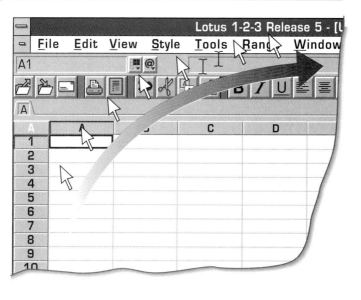

◆ When you move the mouse on your desk, the
mouse pointer (▷ or I) on your screen moves in
the same direction. The mouse pointer changes
shape depending on its location on your screen
and the action you are performing.

7

USING THE MOUSE

PARTS OF THE MOUSE

◆ The mouse has a left and right button. You can use these buttons to:

- open menus
- select commands
- choose options

Note: You will use the left button most of the time.

MOUSE TERMS

CLICK

Quickly press and release the left mouse button once.

DOUBLE-CLICK

Quickly press and release the left mouse button twice.

8

◆ Under the mouse is a ball that senses movement. To ensure smooth motion of the mouse, you should occasionally remove and clean this ball.

DRAG

When the mouse pointer (⬚ or I) is over an object on your screen, press and hold down the left mouse button and then move the mouse.

START 1-2-3

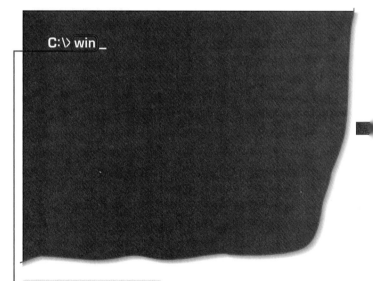

C:\> win_

1 To start 1-2-3 from MS-DOS, type **win** and then press Enter.

When you start 1-2-3, a blank worksheet appears. You can enter data into this worksheet.

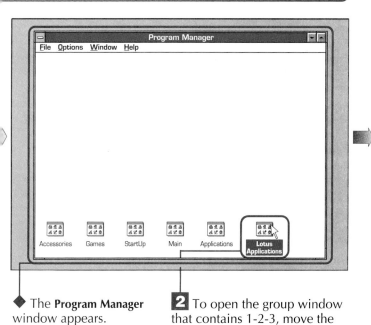

◆ The **Program Manager** window appears.

2 To open the group window that contains 1-2-3, move the mouse ▹ over this icon and then quickly press the left button twice.

To continue, refer to the next page.

START 1-2-3

START 1-2-3 (CONTINUED)

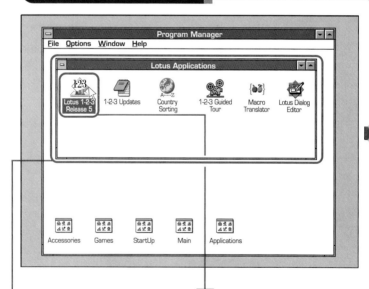

◆ The group window opens.

3 To start the 1-2-3 application, move the mouse ⌖ over this icon and then quickly press the left button twice.

The worksheet displayed on your screen is part of a file. A file is like a three-ring binder that contains several sheets of paper.

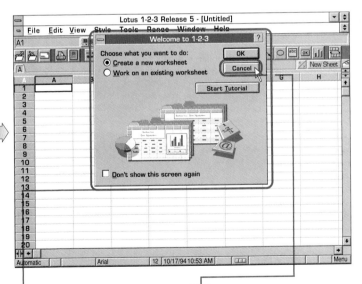

◆ The **Lotus 1-2-3** window appears displaying a blank worksheet. The **Welcome to 1-2-3** dialog box also appears.

4 To close this dialog box, move the mouse ⌖ over **Cancel** and then press the left button.

13

WORKSHEET BASICS

COLUMNS, ROWS AND CELLS

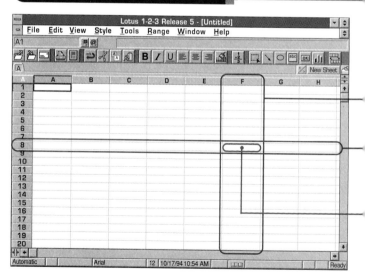

A worksheet consists of columns, rows and cells.

◆ **Column**

A column is a vertical line of boxes. 1-2-3 labels the columns in a worksheet (example: **F**).

◆ **Row**

A row is a horizontal line of boxes. 1-2-3 numbers the rows in a worksheet (example: **8**).

◆ **Cell**

A cell is the area where a column and row intersect (example: **F8**).

THE CURRENT CELL

THE CURRENT CELL

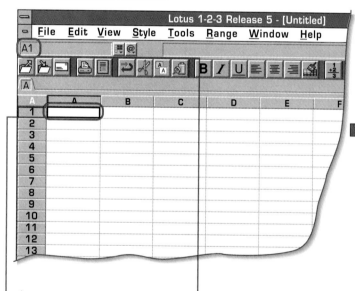

◆ This is the current cell.

◆ This area displays the address (location) of the current cell. An address consists of a column letter followed by a row number (example: **A1**).

The current cell displays a thick border. You can only enter data into the current cell.

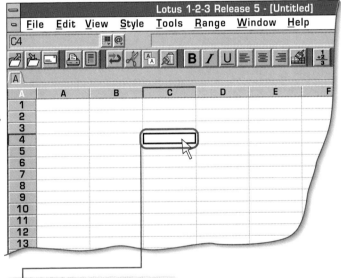

1 To make another cell on your screen the current cell, move the mouse ⊳ over the cell and then press the left button.

◆ The cell now displays a thick border.

17

ENTER DATA

ENTER DATA

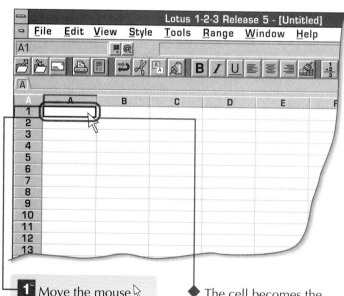

1 Move the mouse ⟍ over the cell where you want to enter data (example: **A1**) and then press the left button.

◆ The cell becomes the current cell and displays a thick border.

18

You use the keyboard to enter data into the cells of your worksheet.

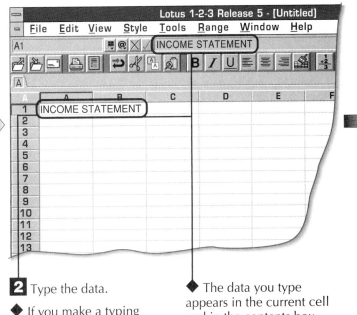

2 Type the data.

◆ If you make a typing error, press **+Backspace** on your keyboard to remove the incorrect data and then retype.

◆ The data you type appears in the current cell and in the contents box.

To continue, refer to the next page.

19

ENTER DATA

Text	**Left Align**
8700	**Right Align**

ENTER DATA (CONTINUED)

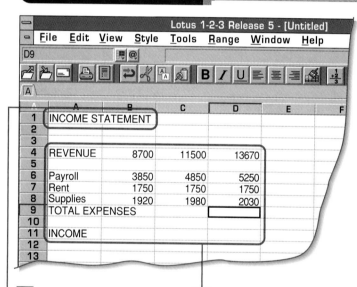

Lotus 1-2-3 Release 5 - [Untitled]

File   Edit   View   Style   Tools   Range   Window   Help

D9

	A	B	C	D	E	F
1	INCOME STATEMENT					
2						
3						
4	REVENUE	8700	11500	13670		
5						
6	Payroll	3850	4850	5250		
7	Rent	1750	1750	1750		
8	Supplies	1920	1980	2030		
9	TOTAL EXPENSES					
10						
11	INCOME					
12						
13						

3 To enter the data, press **Enter**.

or

To enter the data and move one cell in any direction, press **↓**, **↑**, **←** or **→**.

4 Repeat steps **1** to **3** starting on page 18 until you finish entering all your data.

When you enter data in a worksheet, 1-2-3 automatically left aligns text and right aligns numbers.

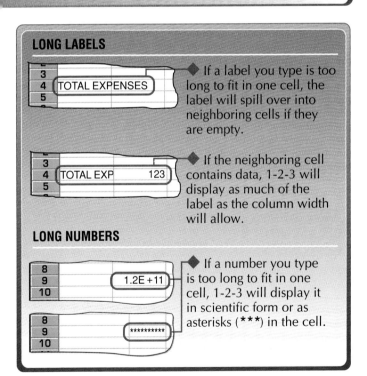

LONG LABELS

◆ If a label you type is too long to fit in one cell, the label will spill over into neighboring cells if they are empty.

◆ If the neighboring cell contains data, 1-2-3 will display as much of the label as the column width will allow.

LONG NUMBERS

◆ If a number you type is too long to fit in one cell, 1-2-3 will display it in scientific form or as asterisks (***) in the cell.

Note: To display an entire label or number, you must increase the column width. For more information, refer to pages 126 to 129.

21

ENTER DATA AUTOMATICALLY

ENTER DATA AUTOMATICALLY

Monday	Tuesday	Wednesday	Thursday
Product1	Product2	Product3	Product4
09:00	10:00	11:00	12:00
1993	1994	1995	1996
1	2	3	4

◆ 1-2-3 completes a series of labels or numbers based on the data in the first cell.

> 1-2-3 can save you time by completing a series of labels or numbers in your worksheet.

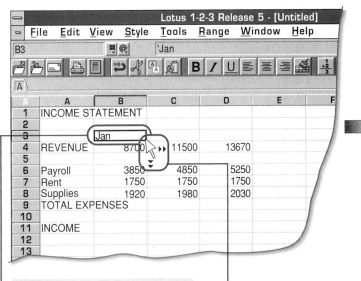

1 Move the mouse ☖ over the cell where you want to enter the first item in the series and then press the left button.

2 Type the first item in the series (example: **Jan**) and then press Enter.

3 Move the mouse ☖ over the bottom right corner of the cell and ☖ changes to ☖".

To continue, refer to the next page.

23

ENTER DATA AUTOMATICALLY

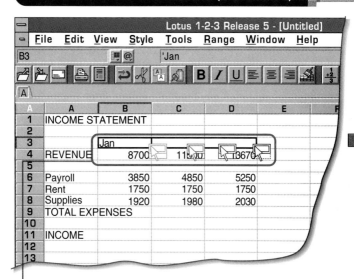

4 Press and hold down the left button as you drag the mouse over the cells you want to include in the series.

This feature is useful if you want to quickly add the months of the year to your worksheet.

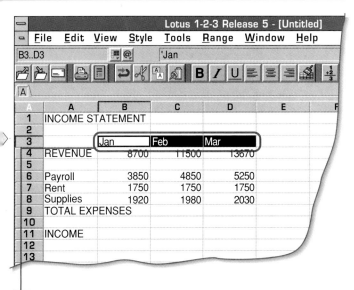

5 Release the button and the cells display the series.

Note: You can also enter data automatically in columns.

SELECT CELLS

SELECT A ROW

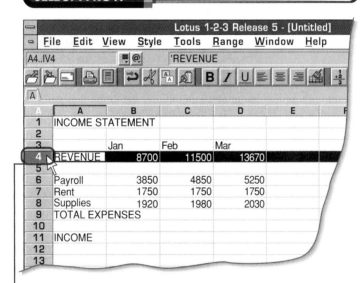

1 Move the mouse ⌖ over the row number you want to select (example: **4**) and then press the left button.

◆ Make sure the mouse looks like ⌖ (not ✛) before pressing the button.

Note: To cancel a selection, move the mouse ⌖ over any cell in your worksheet and then press the left button.

Before you can use many 1-2-3 features, you must first select the cells you want to work with.

SELECT A COLUMN

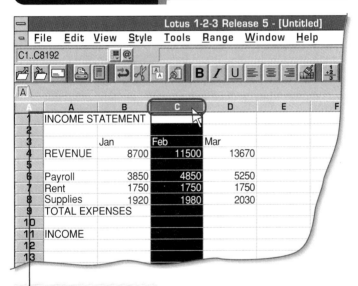

1 Move the mouse ↖ over the column letter you want to select (example: **C**) and then press the left button.

◆ Make sure the mouse looks like ↖ (not ✛) before pressing the button.

SELECT CELLS

SELECT A GROUP OF CELLS

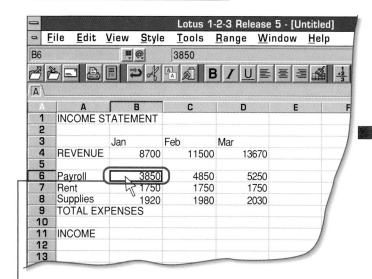

	Lotus 1-2-3 Release 5 - [Untitled]					

File **Edit** **View** **Style** **Tools** **Range** **Window** **Help**

B6   3850

	A	B	C	D	E	F
1	INCOME STATEMENT					
2						
3		Jan	Feb	Mar		
4	REVENUE	8700	11500	13670		
5						
6	Payroll	3850	4850	5250		
7	Rent	1750	1750	1750		
8	Supplies	1920	1980	2030		
9	TOTAL EXPENSES					
10						
11	INCOME					
12						
13						

1 Move the mouse ⍗
over the first cell you want
to select (example: **B6**) and
then press and hold down
the left button.

Selected cells
are called a range
and appear highlighted
on your screen.

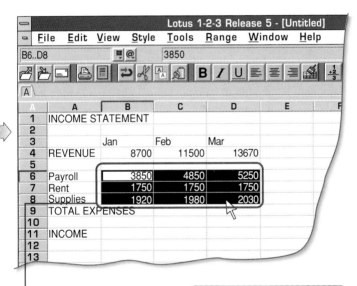

2 Still holding down the
button, drag the mouse
until you highlight all the
cells you want to select.

3 Release the button.

**SELECT TWO
GROUPS OF CELLS**

To select another group
of cells, press and hold
down Ctrl while
repeating steps **1** to **3**.

29

SELECT COMMANDS

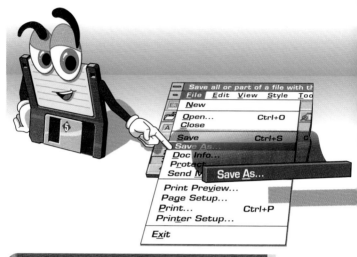

USING THE MENUS WITH THE MOUSE

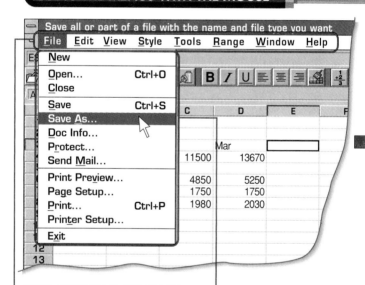

1 To open a menu, move the mouse over the menu name (example: **File**) and then press the left button.

Note: To close a menu, move the mouse over your worksheet and then press the left button.

2 To select a command, move the mouse over the command name (example: **Save As**) and then press the left button.

You can open
a menu to display
a list of related commands.
You can then select the
command you want
to use.

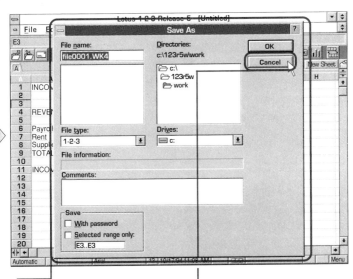

◆ A dialog box appears
if 1-2-3 requires more
information to carry out
the command.

3 To close a dialog box,
move the mouse ↳ over
Cancel and then press the
left button.

SELECT COMMANDS

You can use the keyboard to select a command.

USING THE MENUS WITH THE KEYBOARD

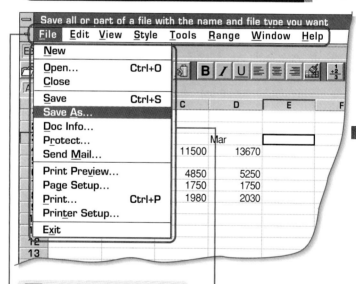

1 To open a menu, press Alt followed by the underlined letter in the menu name (example: F for File).

2 To select a command, press the underlined letter in the command name (example: A for Save As).

Note: To close a menu, press Alt.

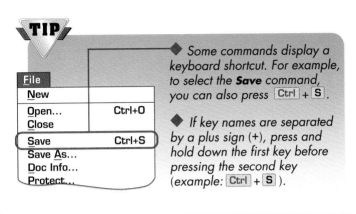

*Some commands display a keyboard shortcut. For example, to select the **Save** command, you can also press `Ctrl` + `S`.*

If key names are separated by a plus sign (+), press and hold down the first key before pressing the second key (example: `Ctrl` + `S`).

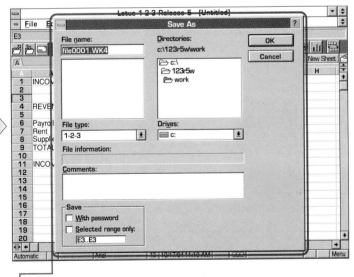

A dialog box appears if 1-2-3 requires more information to carry out the command.

3 To close a dialog box, press `Esc`.

SELECT COMMANDS

USING THE SMARTICONS

Each SmartIcon displayed on your screen provides a fast method of selecting a menu command.

For example, you can use 📁 to quickly select the Save command.

File	
New	
Open...	Ctrl+O
Close	
Save	Ctrl+S
Save As...	
Doc Info...	
Protect...	
Send Mail...	

You can use the SmartIcons to quickly select the most commonly used commands.

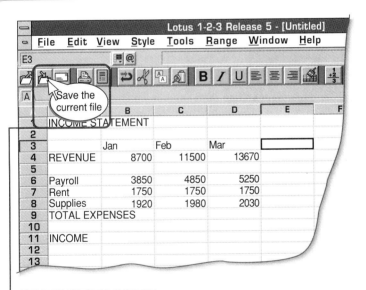

1 Move the mouse ↖ over a SmartIcon of interest (example: 🗁).

◆ A description of the SmartIcon appears.

2 To select the SmartIcon, press the left button.

SELECT COMMANDS

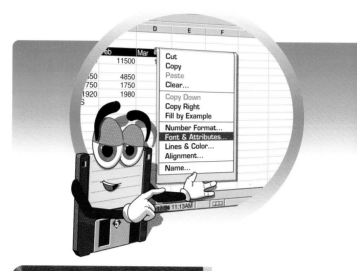

USING THE QUICK MENUS

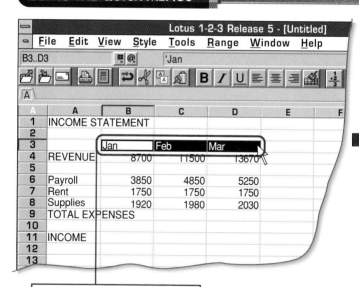

1 Select the cells containing the data you want to work with.

Note: To select cells, refer to pages 26 to 29.

2 Move the mouse ☐ anywhere over the cells you selected and then press the **right** button.

A quick
menu displays
a list of commonly
used commands
for an area you
select.

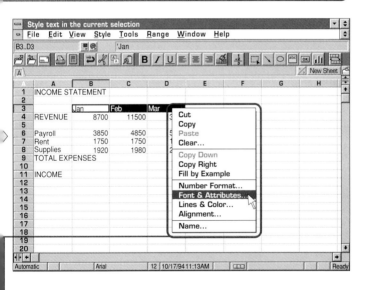

◆ A quick menu appears.

3 Move the mouse ⇱ over the command you want to use and then press the left button.

Note: To close a quick menu, move the mouse ⇱ outside the menu and then press the left button.

MOVE THROUGH A WORKSHEET

MOVE TO CELL A1

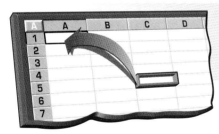

◆ Press **Home** to move to cell **A1** from any cell in your worksheet.

MOVE ONE CELL IN ANY DIRECTION

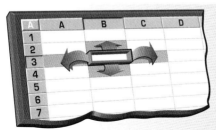

→ Press this key to move **right** one cell.

← Press this key to move **left** one cell.

↓ Press this key to move **down** one cell.

↑ Press this key to move **up** one cell.

If your worksheet contains a lot of data, your computer screen cannot display all of the data at the same time. You must scroll through the worksheet to view other areas.

MOVE ONE SCREEN IN ANY DIRECTION

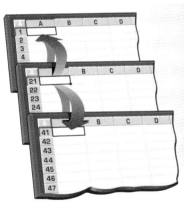

◆ Press **PageDown** to move **down** one screen.

◆ Press **PageUp** to move **up** one screen.

◆ Press **Ctrl** + **→** to move **right** one screen.

◆ Press **Ctrl** + **←** to move **left** one screen.

MOVE THROUGH A WORKSHEET

SCROLL UP OR DOWN

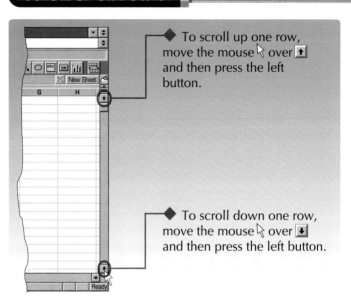

◆ To scroll up one row, move the mouse ⌖ over ▲ and then press the left button.

◆ To scroll down one row, move the mouse ⌖ over ▼ and then press the left button.

SCROLL LEFT OR RIGHT

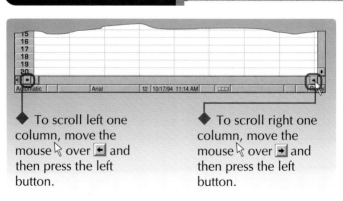

◆ To scroll left one column, move the mouse ⌖ over ◄ and then press the left button.

◆ To scroll right one column, move the mouse ⌖ over ► and then press the left button.

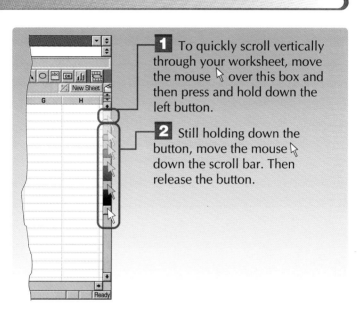

1 To quickly scroll vertically through your worksheet, move the mouse ⟍ over this box and then press and hold down the left button.

2 Still holding down the button, move the mouse ⟍ down the scroll bar. Then release the button.

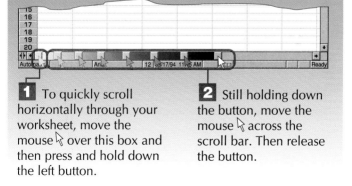

1 To quickly scroll horizontally through your worksheet, move the mouse ⟍ over this box and then press and hold down the left button.

2 Still holding down the button, move the mouse ⟍ across the scroll bar. Then release the button.

GETTING HELP

If you forget how to perform a task, you can use the Help feature to obtain information.

GETTING HELP

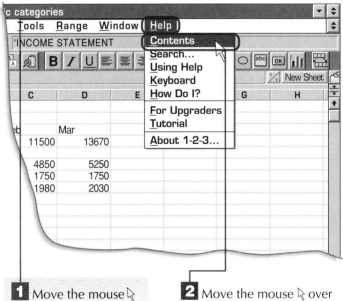

1 Move the mouse ⊳ over **Help** and then press the left button.

2 Move the mouse ⊳ over **Contents** and then press the left button.

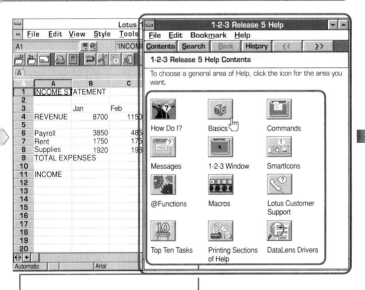

◆ The **1-2-3 Release 5 Help**
window appears.

3 Move the mouse 🖑
over a category of interest
(example: **Basics**) and then
press the left button.

To continue, refer to the next page.

GETTING HELP

The Help feature can save you time by eliminating the need to refer to other sources.

GETTING HELP (CONTINUED)

Basics

Learning About 1-2-3 Release 5

Entering Data

Using the Keyboard

Using the Mouse

Copying, Moving, and Pasting Data

Selecting the Data You Want to Work On

Naming a Worksheet

Enhancing the Appearance of a Worksheet

Creating a Chart

Creating Drawn Objects

Keeping Records in a 1-2-3 Database Table

Setting Up 1-2-3 to Look and Act the Way You Want

Writing a Formula

Printing Data, Drawn Objects, and Help Topics

Top Ten Tasks   Printing Sections of Help   DataLens Drivers

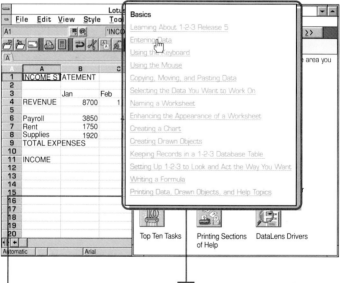

◆ A list of topics in the category you selected appears.

4 Move the mouse over a topic of interest (example: **Entering Data**) and then press the left button.

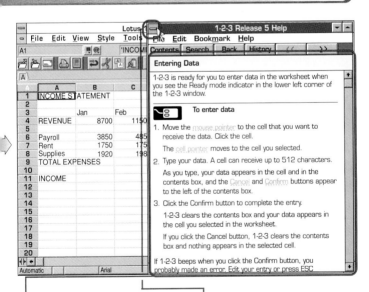

◆ A detailed explanation of the topic you selected appears.

5 To close the **Help** window, move the mouse over ▭ and then quickly press the left button twice.

Your computer stores programs and data in devices called "drives." Like a filing cabinet, a drive stores information in an organized way.

Most computers have one hard drive and one or two floppy drives to store information.

Hard drive (C:)

◆ The hard drive magnetically stores information inside your computer. It is called drive **C**.

*Note: Your computer may be set up to have additional hard drives (example: drive **D**).*

Floppy drives (A: and B:)

◆ A floppy drive stores information on removable diskettes (or floppy disks). A diskette operates slower and stores less data than a hard drive.

◆ **Diskettes are used to:**

- Load new programs.
- Store backup copies of data.
- Transfer data to other computers.

If your computer has only one floppy drive, it is called drive **A**.

If your computer has two floppy drives, the second drive is called drive **B**.

Hard drive (C:)

The hard drive stores your programs and data. It contains many directories to organize your information.

Files

1-2-3 stores your worksheets as files.

Directories

A directory usually contains related information. For example, the **123r5w** directory contains the Lotus 1-2-3 files.

SAVE A FILE

SAVE A FILE

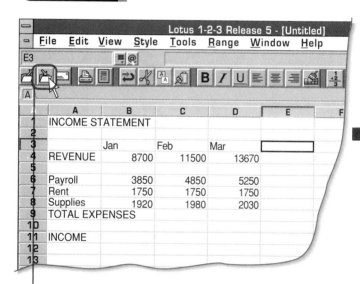

1 Move the mouse ⌖ over 🖫 and then press the left button.

◆ The **Save As** dialog box appears.

*Note: If you previously saved your file, the **Save As** dialog box will **not** appear since you have already named the file.*

50

You should save your file to store it for future use.

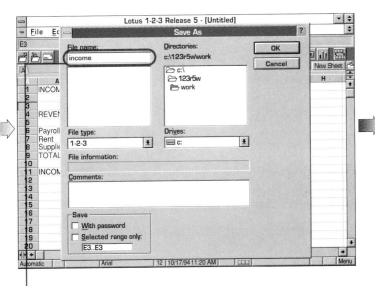

2 Type a name for your file (example: **income**).

◆ To make it easier to find your file later on, do not type an extension. 1-2-3 will automatically add the **wk4** extension to the file name.

To continue, refer to the next page.

51

SAVE A FILE

SAVE A FILE (CONTINUED)

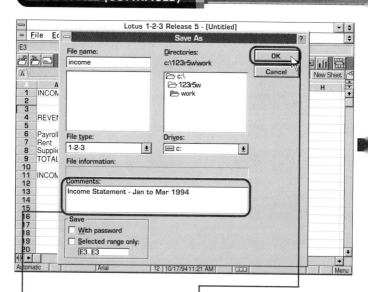

3 To enter information about the file, move the mouse I over this area and then press the left button. Then type the text.

Note: The information you enter will help you identify the file later on.

4 Move the mouse ⤆ over **OK** and then press the left button.

Saving a file lets you later retrieve the file for reviewing or editing purposes.

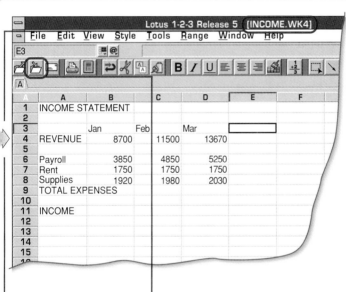

◆ 1-2-3 saves your file and displays the name at the top of your screen.

◆ You should save your file every 5 to 10 minutes to store any changes made since the last time you saved the file. To save changes, move the mouse ⌖ over 🖫 and then press the left button.

53

SAVE A FILE TO A DISKETTE

1 Insert a diskette into a floppy drive (example: **drive a**).

> If you want to give your colleagues a copy of a file, you can save the file to a diskette. They can then review the file on their own computers.

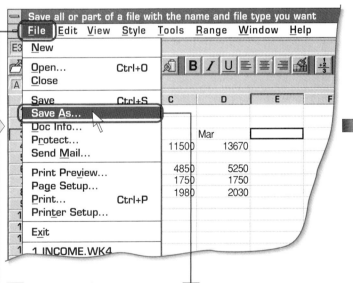

Save all or part of a file with the name and file type you want

| File | Edit | View | Style | Tools | Range | Window | Help |

New

Open...   Ctrl+O
Close

Save   Ctrl+S
Save As...
Doc Info...
Protect...
Send Mail...

Print Preview...
Page Setup...
Print...   Ctrl+P
Printer Setup...

Exit

1 INCOME.WK4

	C	D	E	F
		Mar		
	11500	13670		
	4850	5250		
	1750	1750		
	1980	2030		

2 Move the mouse ▷ over **File** and then press the left button.

3 Move the mouse ▷ over **Save As** and then press the left button.

To continue, refer to the next page.

55

SAVE A FILE TO A DISKETTE

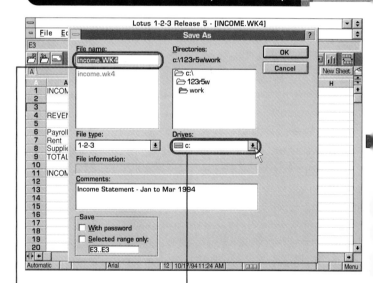

```
─                          Lotus 1-2-3 Release 5 - [INCOME.WK4]              ▼ ◆
▭  File  Ec ─                          Save As                          ?         ◆
E3          File name:                    Directories:              ┌──────────┐
┌──┬──┬──┐  ┌─────────────┐               c:\123r5w\work            │    OK    │  ┌─┬──┬──┐
│  │  │  │  │income.WK4   │                                         └──────────┘  │ │  │  │ New Sheet
┌──┐        └─────────────┘               ┌─ c:\                    ┌──────────┐
│A │ A      income.wk4                     ┌─ 123r5w                │  Cancel  │       H
│1 │ INCOM                                 ┌─ work                  └──────────┘
│2 │
│3 │
│4 │ REVEN
│5 │
│6 │ Payroll   File type:                  Drives:
│7 │ Rent      ┌─────────────┐ ▲           ┌─ c:              ▲
│8 │ Supplie   │1-2-3        │ ▼           └─────────────────┘ ▼
│9 │ TOTAL     File information:                            ▷
│10│
│11│ INCOM
│12│           Comments:
│13│           ┌──────────────────────────────────────┐
│14│           │Income Statement - Jan to Mar 1994      │
│15│           └──────────────────────────────────────┘
│16│          ┌Save────────────────────────────┐
│17│          │ ☐ With password                 │
│18│          │ ☐ Selected range only:          │
│19│          │   ┌───────┐                     │
│20│          │   │E3..E3 │                     │
└──┘          └───┴───────┴─────────────────────┘
Automatic        Arial            12 10/17/94 11:24 AM                       Menu
```

◆ The **Save As** dialog box appears.

4 The **File name:** box displays the current file name. To save your file with a different name, type a new name.

◆ The **Drives:** box displays the current drive (example: **c:**).

5 To save the file to a different drive, move the mouse ▷ over ▼ in the **Drives:** box and then press the left button.

As a precaution, you should save your file to a diskette. You can then use this copy to replace any lost data if your hard drive fails or you accidentally erase the file.

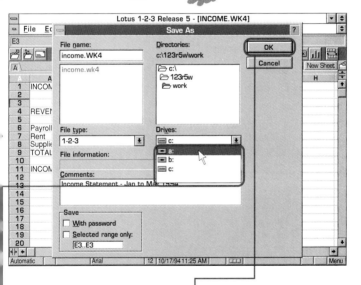

◆ A list of the available drives for your computer appears.

6 Move the mouse ⬚ over the drive you want to use (example: **a:**) and then press the left button.

7 To save your file, move the mouse ⬚ over **OK** and then press the left button.

57

EXIT 1-2-3

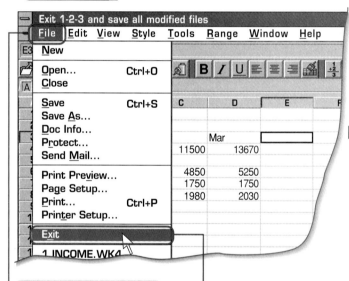

1 Move the mouse ⌖ over **File** and then press the left button.

2 Move the mouse ⌖ over **Exit** and then press the left button.

When you
finish using 1-2-3,
you can exit the program
to return to the Windows
Program Manager.

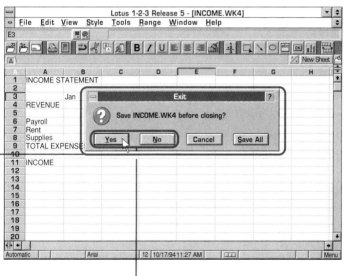

◆ This dialog box
appears if you have
not saved changes
made to your file.

3 To save your file before exiting,
move the mouse ⟍ over **Yes** and
then press the left button.

↳◆ To exit without saving your file,
move the mouse ⟍ over **No** and
then press the left button.

OPEN A FILE

OPEN A FILE

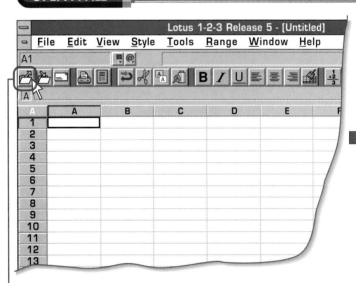

1 Move the mouse ⌖ over 🗀 and then press the left button.

◆ The **Open File** dialog box appears.

60

You can open a saved file and display it on your screen.

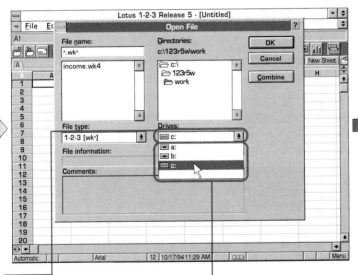

◆ The **Drives:** box displays the current drive (example: **c:**).

2 To open a file on a different drive, move the mouse ⌖ over ⬇ in the **Drives:** box and then press the left button.

3 Move the mouse ⌖ over the drive containing the file you want to open and then press the left button.

To continue, refer to the next page.

61

OPEN A FILE

OPEN A FILE (CONTINUED)

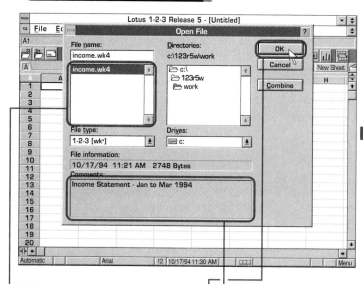

4 Move the mouse ⌖ over the name of the file you want to open (example: **income.wk4**) and then press the left button.

◆ This area displays the text you entered when you saved the file.

5 Move the mouse ⌖ over **OK** and then press the left button.

Once you open a file, you can review and edit your work.

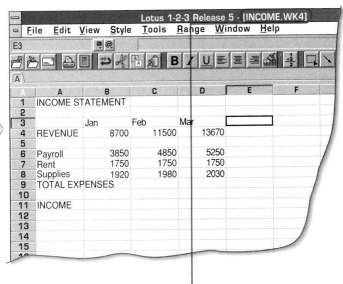

```
                    Lotus 1-2-3 Release 5 - [INCOME.WK4]
  File   Edit   View   Style   Tools   Range   Window   Help
E3                @
┌──────────────────────────────────────────────────────────┐
│  B  I  U  ≡ ≡ ≡              +2/3
A
      A           B         C         D        E         F
 1   INCOME STATEMENT
 2
 3                Jan       Feb       Mar
 4   REVENUE      8700      11500     13670
 5
 6   Payroll      3850      4850      5250
 7   Rent         1750      1750      1750
 8   Supplies     1920      1980      2030
 9   TOTAL EXPENSES
10
11   INCOME
12
13
14
15
```

◆ 1-2-3 opens the file and displays it on your screen. You can now make changes to the file.

◆ The name of the file appears at the top of your screen.

OPEN A FILE

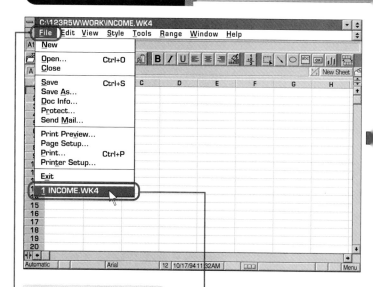

1 Move the mouse ⬚ over **File** and then press the left button.

2 Move the mouse ⬚ over the name of the file you want to open and then press the left button.

Note: In this example, only one file has been opened.

The File menu displays the names of the last five files you opened. You can easily open one of these files.

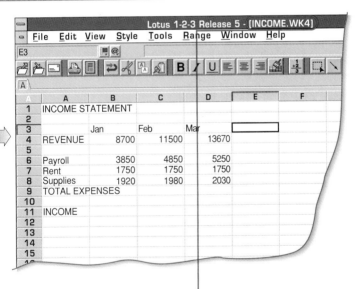

◆ 1-2-3 opens the file and displays it on your screen. You can now make changes to the file.

◆ The name of the file appears at the top of your screen.

EDIT DATA IN A CELL

EDIT DATA IN A CELL

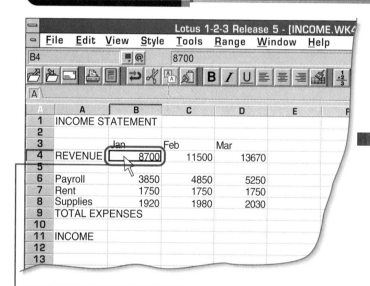

1 Move the mouse over the cell containing the data you want to change (example: **B4**) and then quickly press the left button twice.

After you enter data into your worksheet, you can correct a typing error or revise the data.

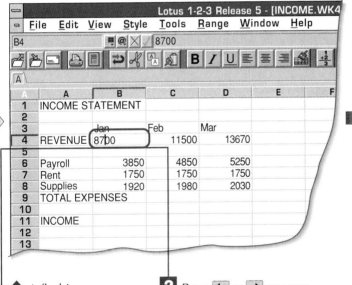

Lotus 1-2-3 Release 5 - [INCOME.WK4

File Edit View Style Tools Range Window Help

B4   ▪ @ ✕ ✓ 8700

	A	B	C	D	E	F
1	INCOME STATEMENT					
2						
3		Jan	Feb	Mar		
4	REVENUE	87|00	11500	13670		
5						
6	Payroll	3850	4850	5250		
7	Rent	1750	1750	1750		
8	Supplies	1920	1980	2030		
9	TOTAL EXPENSES					
10						
11	INCOME					
12						
13						

◆ A flashing insertion point appears in the cell.

2 Press ← or → on your keyboard to move the insertion point where you want to add or delete characters.

To continue, refer to the next page.

EDIT DATA IN A CELL

EDIT DATA IN A CELL (CONTINUED)

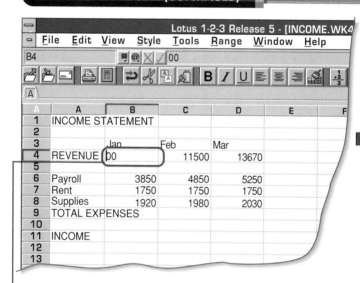

Lotus 1-2-3 Release 5 - [INCOME.WK4

| File | Edit | View | Style | Tools | Range | Window | Help |

B4   @ X √ 00

	A	B	C	D	E	F
1	INCOME STATEMENT					
2						
3		Jan	Feb	Mar		
4	REVENUE	00	11500	13670		
5						
6	Payroll	3850	4850	5250		
7	Rent	1750	1750	1750		
8	Supplies	1920	1980	2030		
9	TOTAL EXPENSES					
10						
11	INCOME					
12						
13						

3 To remove the character to the left of the insertion point, press ◆Backspace.

◆ To remove the character to the right of the insertion point, press Delete.

68

REPLACE ENTIRE CELL CONTENTS

You can completely replace the contents of a cell with new data.

1 Move the mouse ⬉ over the cell containing the data you want to replace with new data and then press the left button.

2 Type the new data and then press `Enter`.

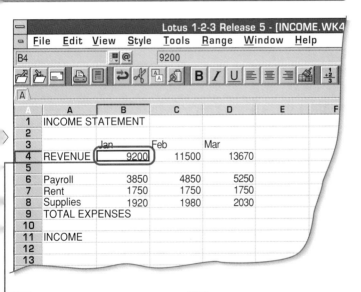

4 To insert data where the insertion point flashes on your screen, type the data.

5 When you finish making the changes, press `Enter`.

69

DELETE DATA

DELETE DATA

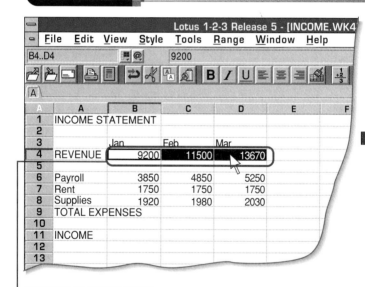

1 Select the cells containing the data you want to remove.

Note: To select cells, refer to pages 26 to 29.

> You can completely erase the contents of cells in your worksheet.

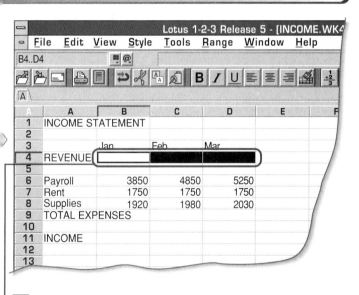

2 Press **Delete** and the data in the cells you selected disappears.

71

UNDO LAST CHANGE

> 1-2-3 remembers the last change you made to your worksheet. If you regret this change, you can cancel it by immediately using the Undo feature.

UNDO YOUR LAST CHANGE

```
                              Lotus 1-2-3 Release 5 - [INCOME.WK4
  File   Edit   View   Style   Tools   Range   Window   Help
B4..D4              @
```

	A	B	C	D	E	F
1	INCOME STATEMENT					
2						
3		Jan	Feb	Mar		
4	REVENUE					
5						
6	Payroll	3850	4850	5250		
7	Rent	1750	1750	1750		
8	Supplies	1920	1980	2030		
9	TOTAL EXPENSES					
10						
11	INCOME					
12						
13						

1 To cancel the last change made to your worksheet, move the mouse ⬚ over ⬚ and then press the left button.

Lotus 1-2-3 Release 5 - [INCOME.WK4

| File | Edit | View | Style | Tools | Range | Window | Help |

B4   @   9200

A	A	B	C	D	E	F
1	INCOME STATEMENT					
2						
3		Jan	Feb	Mar		
4	REVENUE	9200	11500	13670		
5						
6	Payroll	3850	4850	5250		
7	Rent	1750	1750	1750		
8	Supplies	1920	1980	2030		
9	TOTAL EXPENSES					
10						
11	INCOME					
12						
13						

◆ 1-2-3 cancels
your last change.

*Note: In this example, 1-2-3
restores the data you deleted.*

73

MOVE DATA

DRAG AND DROP DATA

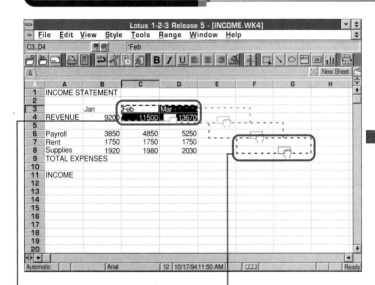

1 Select the cells containing the data you want to move to a new location.

Note: To select cells, refer to pages 26 to 29.

2 Move the mouse ⟨ over a border of the selected cells (⟨ changes to ⟨ᵐ⟩).

3 Press and hold down the left button as you drag the mouse ⟨ᵐ⟩ where you want to place the data.

◆ A dotted rectangular box indicates where the data will appear.

74

You can move data from one location in your worksheet to another. This lets you reorganize the data in your worksheet.

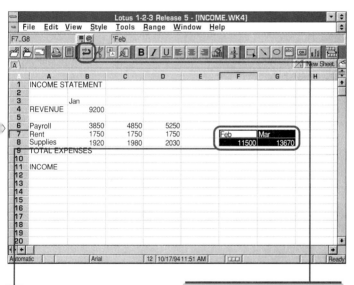

4 Release the left button and the data moves to the new location.

CANCEL THE MOVE

◆ To immediately cancel the move, position the mouse ▷ over 🔁 and then press the left button.

MOVE DATA

CUT AND PASTE DATA

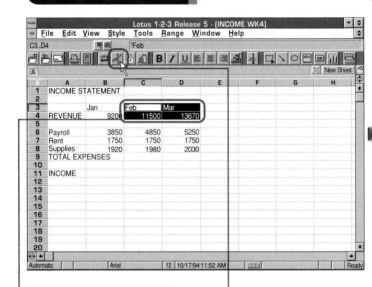

1 Select the cells containing the data you want to move to a new location.

Note: To select cells, refer to pages 26 to 29.

2 Move the mouse ⇗ over ✂ and then press the left button.

◆ The data disappears from your screen.

To move data
to a new location in
your worksheet,
you can use the
Cut and Paste
SmartIcons.

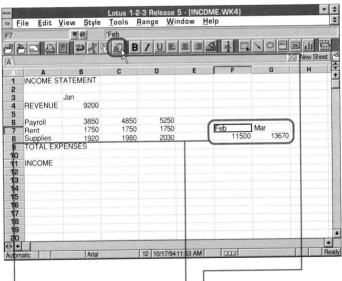

3 Select the cell where
you want to place the
data. This cell will
become the top left
cell of the new location.

4 Move the mouse ⌖
over 🖾 and then press
the left button.

◆ The data appears in
the new location.

COPY DATA

DRAG AND DROP DATA

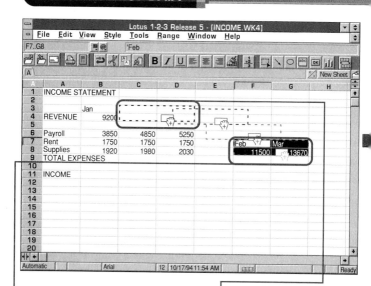

1 Select the cells containing the data you want to copy to a new location.

Note: To select cells, refer to pages 26 to 29.

2 Move the mouse ⫢ over a border of the selected cells (⫢ changes to 🖑).

3 Press and hold down **Ctrl** and the left button as you drag the mouse 🖑 where you want to place the copy.

◆ A dotted rectangular box indicates where the data will appear.

78

> Like a photocopy machine, you can make an exact copy of data and then place the copy in a new location.

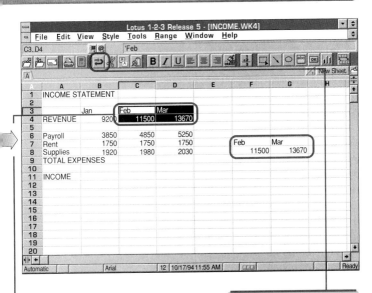

4 Release the left button and then release **Ctrl**.

◆ A copy of the data appears in the new location.

CANCEL THE COPY

◆ To immediately cancel the copy, move the mouse over ↰ and then press the left button.

COPY DATA

COPY AND PASTE DATA

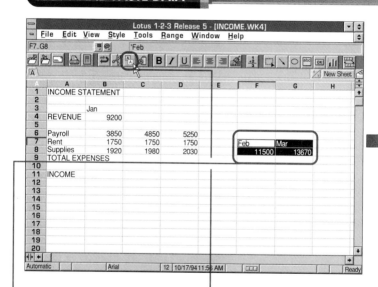

1 Select the cells containing the data you want to copy to a new location.

Note: To select cells, refer to pages 26 to 29.

2 Move the mouse ⬚ over 🔲 and then press the left button.

To place
a copy of your data
in a new location,
you can use the
Copy and Paste
SmartIcons.

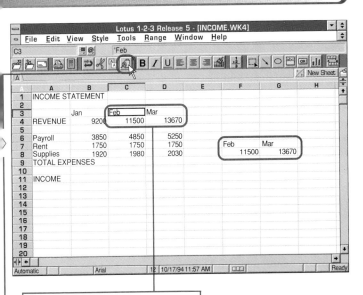

3 Select the cell where you want to place the data. This cell will become the top left cell of the new location.

4 Move the mouse ⍀ over 🖾 and then press the left button.

◆ A copy of the data appears in the new location.

*Note: You can repeat steps **3** and **4** to place the data in multiple locations in your worksheet.*

81

CHECK SPELLING

You can use the Spelling feature to find and correct spelling errors in your worksheet.

Lotus Dictionary
Expanded 5.0 Version

CHECK SPELLING

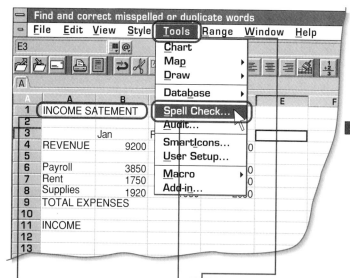

Find and correct misspelled or duplicate words

| File | Edit | View | Style | **Tools** | Range | Window | Help |

E3

	A	B			E	F
1	INCOME SATEMENT					
2						
3		Jan				
4	REVENUE	9200			0	
5						
6	Payroll	3850			0	
7	Rent	1750			0	
8	Supplies	1920			0	
9	TOTAL EXPENSES					
10						
11	INCOME					
12						
13						

Tools menu:
Chart
Map
Draw
Database
Spell Check...
Audit...
SmartIcons...
User Setup...
Macro
Add-in...

◆ In this example, the first letter **T** was removed from **STATEMENT**.

Note: To spell check a section of your worksheet, select the cells before performing step **1**. *To select cells, refer to pages 26 to 29.*

1 Move the mouse over **Tools** and then press the left button.

2 Move the mouse over **Spell Check** and then press the left button.

82

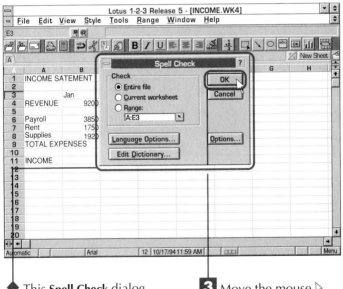

◆ This **Spell Check** dialog box appears.

3 Move the mouse ⌖ over **OK** and then press the left button.

To continue, refer to the next page.

83

CHECK SPELLING

1-2-3 compares every word in your worksheet to words in its own dictionary. If a word does not exist in the dictionary, 1-2-3 considers it misspelled.

Lotus Dictionary
Expanded 5.0 Version

CHECK SPELLING (CONTINUED)

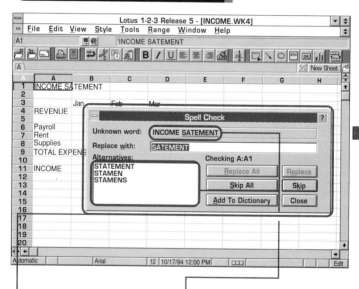

◆ If 1-2-3 finds a spelling error, this **Spell Check** dialog box appears.

◆ 1-2-3 displays the word it does not recognize and suggestions to correct the error.

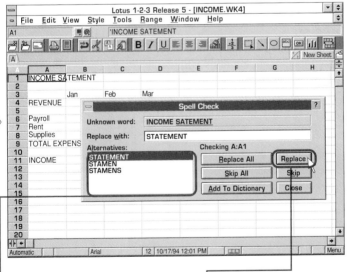

Correct misspelled word

4 To correct the spelling, move the mouse ⌖ over the word you want to use and then press the left button.

5 Move the mouse ⌖ over **Replace** and then press the left button.

To continue, refer to the next page.

85

CHECK SPELLING

This dialog box appears when the spell check is complete.

CHECK SPELLING (CONTINUED)

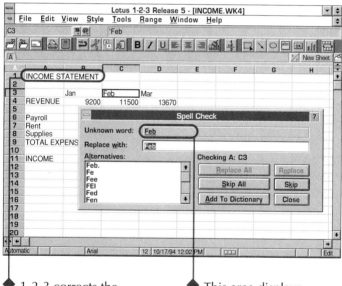

◆ 1-2-3 corrects the word and continues checking for spelling errors.

◆ This area displays the next word 1-2-3 does not recognize.

◆ To close the dialog box, move the mouse ▷ over **OK** and then press the left button.

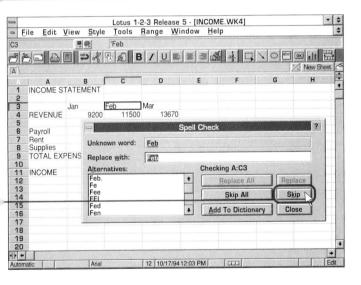

Skip misspelled word

6 If you do not want to change the spelling of the word, move the mouse ▷ over **Skip** and then press the left button.

◆ Correct or skip spelling errors until 1-2-3 finishes checking your worksheet.

87

FORMULAS

INTRODUCTION TO FORMULAS

You can use these operators in your formulas:

+	Addition
-	Subtraction
*	Multiplication
/	Division
^	Exponentiation

◆ You must begin a formula with a plus sign (+).

◆ You should use cell addresses (example: **A1**) instead of actual numbers whenever possible. This way, if your data changes, 1-2-3 will automatically redo the calculations.

> You can use formulas to perform calculations on your worksheet data.

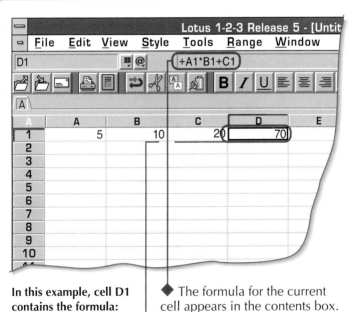

In this example, cell **D1** contains the formula:

+A1*B1+C1

=5*10+20

=70

◆ The formula for the current cell appears in the contents box.

◆ The result of the calculation appears in the cell containing the formula (example: **D1**).

89

FORMULAS

INTRODUCTION TO FORMULAS

1-2-3 will perform calculations in the following order:

1 Exponentiation

2 Multiplication and Division

3 Addition and Subtraction

You can change this order by using parentheses ( ).

1-2-3 performs all of your calculations in a specific order.

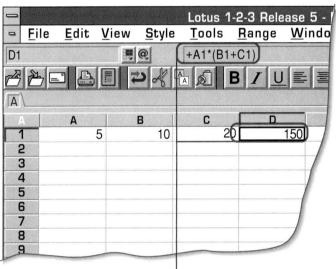

1-2-3 will calculate the numbers in parentheses first.

◆ In this example, cell D1 contains the formula:

+A1*(B1+C1)

=5*(10+20)

=150

91

ENTER A FORMULA

ENTER A FORMULA

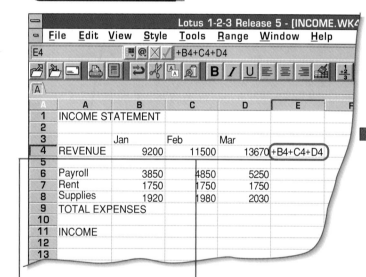

1 Move the mouse over the cell where you want to enter a formula and then press the left button.

2 Type a plus sign (+) to begin the formula.

3 Type the calculation you want to perform (example: **B4+C4+D4**).

Note: This formula will calculate the total Revenue.

> You can enter a formula into any cell in your worksheet.

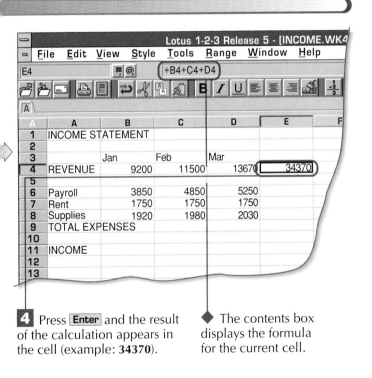

Lotus 1-2-3 Release 5 - [INCOME.WK4

File   Edit   View   Style   Tools   Range   Window   Help

E4   +B4+C4+D4

	A	B	C	D	E	F
1	INCOME STATEMENT					
2						
3		Jan	Feb	Mar		
4	REVENUE	9200	11500	13670	34370	
5						
6	Payroll	3850	4850	5250		
7	Rent	1750	1750	1750		
8	Supplies	1920	1980	2030		
9	TOTAL EXPENSES					
10						
11	INCOME					
12						
13						

4 Press **Enter** and the result of the calculation appears in the cell (example: **34370**).

◆ The contents box displays the formula for the current cell.

AUTOMATIC RECALCULATION

AUTOMATIC RECALCULATION

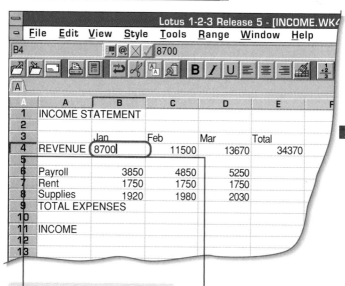

	Lotus 1-2-3 Release 5 - [INCOME.WK4

File Edit View Style Tools Range Window Help

B4   @ × ✓ 8700

A	A	B	C	D	E	F
1	INCOME STATEMENT					
2						
3		Jan	Feb	Mar	Total	
4	REVENUE	8700	11500	13670	34370	
5						
6	Payroll	3850	4850	5250		
7	Rent	1750	1750	1750		
8	Supplies	1920	1980	2030		
9	TOTAL EXPENSES					
10						
11	INCOME					
12						
13						

1 Move the mouse ⟶ over the cell you want to change (example: **B4**) and then press the left button.

2 Type a new number (example: **8700**).

If you change a number used in a formula, 1-2-3 will automatically calculate a new result.

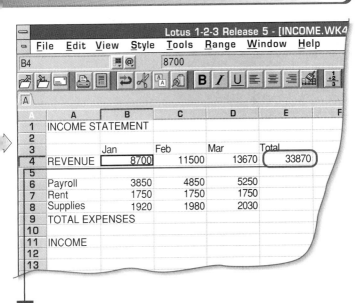

3 Press **Enter** and 1-2-3 automatically recalculates the formula using the new number.

95

FUNCTIONS

INTRODUCTION TO FUNCTIONS

◆ A function starts with the @ symbol.

◆ You should use cell addresses (example: **A1**) instead of actual numbers whenever possible. This way, if your data changes, 1-2-3 will automatically redo the calculations.

A function is a ready-to-use formula. 1-2-3 offers over 200 functions to perform specialized calculations on your worksheet data.

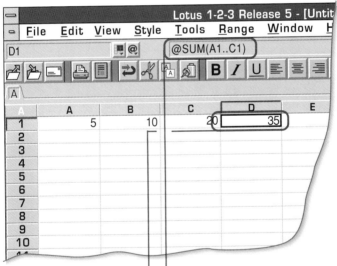

In this example, cell D1 contains the function:
@SUM(A1..C1)
=A1+B1+C1
=5+10+20
=35

◆ The function for the current cell appears in the contents box.

◆ The result of the calculation appears in the cell containing the function (example: **D1**).

97

FUNCTIONS

You must tell 1-2-3 which data you want to use
to calculate a function. The data is enclosed in
parentheses ( ).

@SUM(A1,A3,A5)

◆ When there is a comma (,) between
cell addresses in a function, 1-2-3 uses
each cell to perform the calculation.

*Example: @SUM(A1,A3,A5) is the same as the
formula +A1+A3+A5.*

@SUM(A1..A4)

◆ When there are two periods (..)
between cell addresses in a function,
1-2-3 uses the displayed cells and all
cells between them to perform the
calculation.

*Example: @SUM(A1..A4) is the same as the formula
+A1+A2+A3+A4.*

Common Functions

AVG   Calculates the average value of a list of numbers.
Example: @AVG(B1..B6)

COUNT   Counts the number of values in a list of numbers.
Example: @COUNT(B1..B6)

MAX   Finds the largest value in a list of numbers.
Example: @MAX(B1..B6)

MIN   Finds the smallest value in a list of numbers.
Example: @MIN(B1..B6)

ROUND   Rounds a number to a specific number of digits.
Example: @ROUND(B6,2)

SUM   Adds a list of numbers.
Example: @SUM(B1..B6)

ENTER A FUNCTION

ENTER A FUNCTION

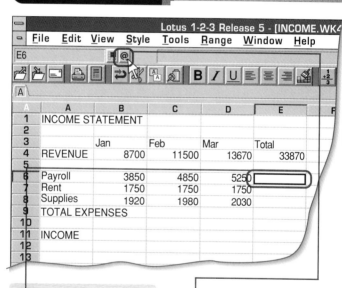

1 Move the mouse ⌖ over the cell where you want to enter a function and then press the left button.

2 Move the mouse ⌖ over @ and then press the left button.

> Functions
> let you perform
> calculations without
> having to type complex
> formulas.

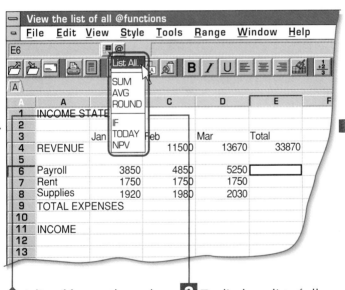

◆ A list of frequently used functions appears.

Note: If the function you want to use appears in this list, move the mouse ▷ over the function and then press the left button. Then skip to step 6 on page 104.

3 To display a list of all the functions, move the mouse ▷ over **List All** and then press the left button.

To continue, refer to the next page.

ENTER A FUNCTION

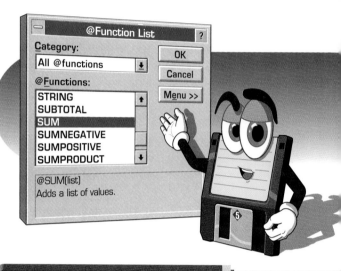

@SUM(list)
Adds a list of values.

ENTER A FUNCTION (CONTINUED)

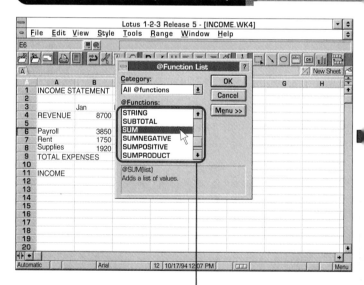

◆ The **@Function List** dialog box appears.

4 Move the mouse ▷ over the function you want to use (example: **SUM**) and then press the left button.

Note: To view all of the available functions, use the scroll bar. For more information, refer to page 40.

You can select from hundreds of functions to perform tasks such as averaging a group of numbers or calculating mortgage payments.

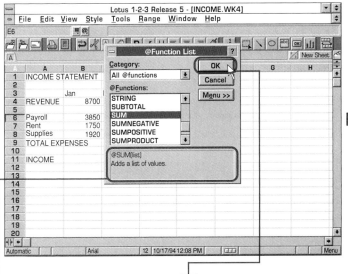

◆ This area displays a description of the function you selected.

5 To select this function, move the mouse ↳ over **OK** and then press the left button.

To continue, refer to the next page.

103

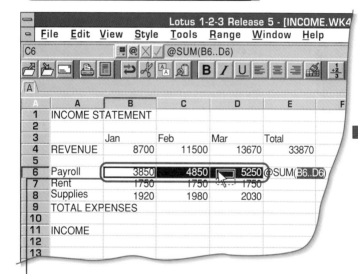

6 Select the cells containing the data you want to use in the function.

Note: To select cells, refer to pages 26 to 29.

◆ You can also type the cell addresses you want to use. Make sure you separate each cell address with a comma (example: **B6,C6,D6**).

If you change a number used in a function, 1-2-3 will automatically calculate a new result.

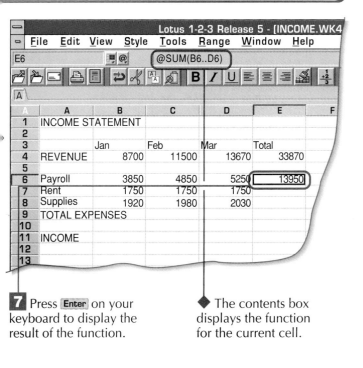

Lotus 1-2-3 Release 5 - [INCOME.WK4

File   Edit   View   Style   Tools   Range   Window   Help

E6   @SUM(B6..D6)

	A	B	C	D	E	F
1	INCOME STATEMENT					
2						
3		Jan	Feb	Mar	Total	
4	REVENUE	8700	11500	13670	33870	
5						
6	Payroll	3850	4850	5250	13950	
7	Rent	1750	1750	1750		
8	Supplies	1920	1980	2030		
9	TOTAL EXPENSES					
10						
11	INCOME					
12						
13						

7 Press **Enter** on your keyboard to display the result of the function.

◆ The contents box displays the function for the current cell.

ADD NUMBERS

ADD A LIST OF NUMBERS

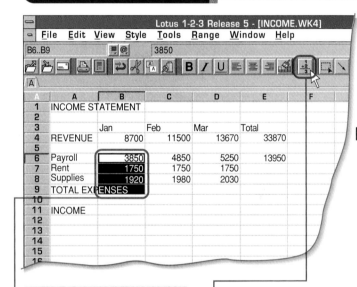

	A	B	C	D	E	F
1	INCOME STATEMENT					
2						
3		Jan	Feb	Mar	Total	
4	REVENUE	8700	11500	13670	33870	
5						
6	Payroll	3850	4850	5250	13950	
7	Rent	1750	1750	1750		
8	Supplies	1920	1980	2030		
9	TOTAL EXPENSES					
10						
11	INCOME					
12						
13						
14						
15						
16						

1 Select the cells containing the numbers you want to sum, including a blank cell for the result.

Note: To select cells, refer to pages 26 to 29.

2 Move the mouse ⌖ over ⊞ and then press the left button.

You can use the Sum SmartIcon to quickly add a list of numbers in your worksheet.

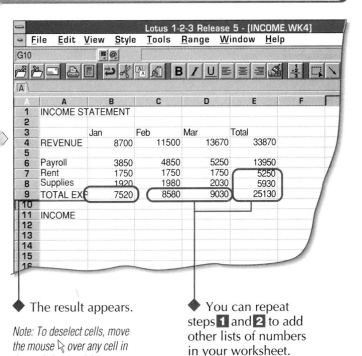

	Lotus 1-2-3 Release 5 - [INCOME.WK4]					
File	Edit	View	Style	Tools	Range	Window	Help

G10

	A	B	C	D	E	F
1	INCOME STATEMENT					
2						
3		Jan	Feb	Mar	Total	
4	REVENUE	8700	11500	13670	33870	
5						
6	Payroll	3850	4850	5250	13950	
7	Rent	1750	1750	1750	5250	
8	Supplies	1920	1980	2030	5930	
9	TOTAL EXP	7520	8580	9030	25130	
10						
11	INCOME					
12						
13						
14						
15						
16						

◆ The result appears.

Note: To deselect cells, move the mouse ⩥ over any cell in the worksheet and then press the left button.

◆ You can repeat steps 1 and 2 to add other lists of numbers in your worksheet.

ERRORS IN FORMULAS

COMMON ERRORS IN FORMULAS

A	A	B	C	D
1	5		50	
2	10			
3	ERR		ERR	
4				

This cell contains the formula +A1+A

A formula must contain cell addresses that 1-2-3 recognizes.

Note: Make sure you look for typing errors when correcting formulas.

This cell contains the formula +C1/C2 = 50/0

A formula cannot divide a number by 0. 1-2-3 considers a blank cell to contain the zero value.

An error message appears when 1-2-3 cannot properly calculate a formula. You can correct an error by editing the cell displaying the error message.

CORRECT AN ERROR

1 To correct an error, move the mouse ⬚ over the cell displaying the error message and then quickly press the left button twice.

2 Edit the formula as you would any data in your worksheet.

Note: To edit data, refer to pages 66 to 69.

COPY FORMULAS

After entering a formula in your worksheet, you can copy the formula to other cells.

COPY FORMULAS (USING RELATIVE REFERENCES)

When you copy a formula, 1-2-3 automatically changes the cell addresses in the new formulas.

A	A	B	C	D
1	10	20	5	
2	20	30	10	
3	30	40	20	
4	60	90	35	
5				
6				

+A1+A2+A3 ➡ +B1+B2+B3   +C1+C2+C3

This cell contains the formula +A1+A2+A3

If you copy the formula to other cells in the worksheet, the cell addresses in the new formulas automatically change.

USING FORMULAS AND FUNCTIONS

Lotus 1-2-3 Release 5 - [INCOME.WK4]

File Edit View Style Tools Range Window Help

B11   +B4-B9

	A	B	C	D	E	F
1	INCOME STATEMENT					
2						
3		Jan	Feb	Mar	Total	
4	REVENUE	8700	11500	13670	33870	
5						
6	Payroll	3850	4850	5250	13950	
7	Rent	1750	1750	1750	5250	
8	Supplies	1920	1980	2030	5930	
9	TOTAL EXF	7520	8580	9030	25130	
10						
11	INCOME	1180				
12						
13						
14						
15						
16						

1 Enter the formula you want to copy to other cells (example: to calculate INCOME, enter **+B4-B9** in cell **B11**).

2 Move the mouse ⬡ over the cell containing the formula and then press the left button.

To continue, refer to the next page.

111

COPY FORMULAS

COPY FORMULAS (CONTINUED)

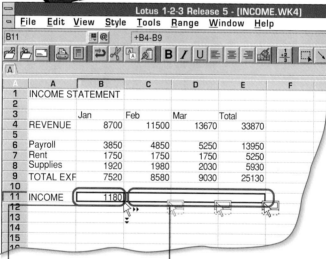

Lotus 1-2-3 Release 5 - [INCOME.WK4]

File Edit View Style Tools Range Window Help

B11   +B4-B9

	A	B	C	D	E	F
1	INCOME STATEMENT					
2						
3		Jan	Feb	Mar	Total	
4	REVENUE	8700	11500	13670	33870	
5						
6	Payroll	3850	4850	5250	13950	
7	Rent	1750	1750	1750	5250	
8	Supplies	1920	1980	2030	5930	
9	TOTAL EXF	7520	8580	9030	25130	
10						
11	INCOME	1180				
12						
13						
14						
15						

3 Move the mouse �
over the bottom right
corner of the cell and
☐ changes to ☝".

4 Press and hold down
the left button as you drag
the mouse ▱ over the
cells you want to receive
a copy of the formula.

Copying a formula saves you time when entering the same formula into several cells.

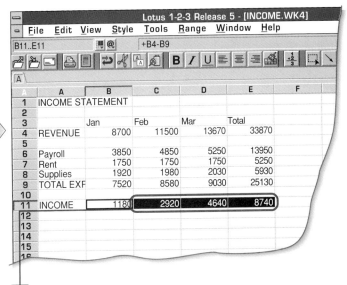

5 Release the button and the results of the formulas appear.

COPY FORMULAS

To make a cell reference absolute, type a dollar sign ($) before both the column letter and row number (example: $B$1).

A	A	B	C	D	E
1	Cost per item	10			
2					
3	Number of items	10	20	30	
4	Total Cost	100	200	300	
5					
6					
7					

+$B$1*B3 ➡ +$B$1*C3   +$B$1*D3

This cell contains the formula +$B$1*B3

If you copy the formula to other cells in the worksheet, the cell address B1 does not change in the new formulas.

To save time, you can copy a formula to other cells in your worksheet. If you do not want 1-2-3 to change a cell address when copying the formula, you must lock the cell. A locked cell address is called an absolute reference.

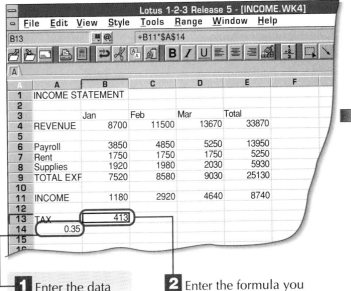

Lotus 1-2-3 Release 5 - [INCOME.WK4]

File   Edit   View   Style   Tools   Range   Window   Help

B13   @   +B11*$A$14

	A	B	C	D	E	F
1	INCOME STATEMENT					
2						
3		Jan	Feb	Mar	Total	
4	REVENUE	8700	11500	13670	33870	
5						
6	Payroll	3850	4850	5250	13950	
7	Rent	1750	1750	1750	5250	
8	Supplies	1920	1980	2030	5930	
9	TOTAL EXP	7520	8580	9030	25130	
10						
11	INCOME	1180	2920	4640	8740	
12						
13	TAX	413				
14	0.35					
15						

1 Enter the data you want to use as an absolute cell reference (example: **0.35** in cell **A14**).

2 Enter the formula you want to copy to other cells (example: to calculate TAX, enter **+B11*$A$14** in cell **B13**).

To continue, refer to the next page.

115

COPY FORMULAS

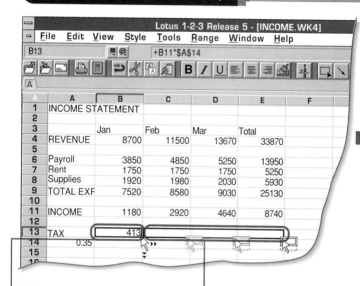

3 Move the mouse ⓝ over the cell containing the formula you want to copy (example: **B13**) and then press the left button.

4 Move the mouse ⓝ over the bottom right corner of the cell and ⓝ changes to ⓝ⁺.

5 Press and hold down the left button as you drag the mouse ⓝ over the cells you want to receive a copy of the formula.

116

An absolute reference always refers to the same cell, regardless of where you copy the formula.

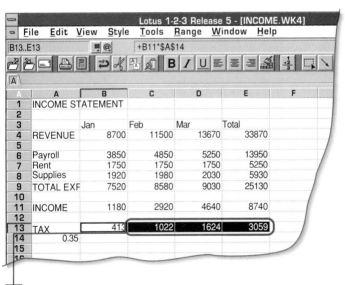

6 Release the button and the results of the formulas appear.

INSERT A ROW

INSERT A ROW

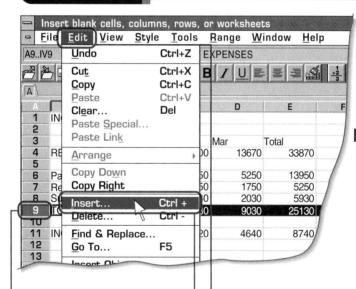

A new row will appear above the row you select.

1 To select a row, move the mouse ⧖ over the row heading (example: **row 9**) and then press the left button.

2 Move the mouse ⧖ over **Edit** and then press the left button.

3 Move the mouse ⧖ over **Insert** and then press the left button.

118

You can add a row to your worksheet if you want to insert new data.

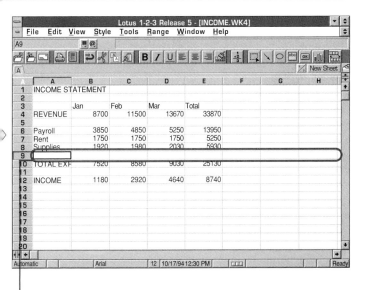

◆ The new row appears and all the rows that follow shift downward.

INSERT A COLUMN

INSERT A COLUMN

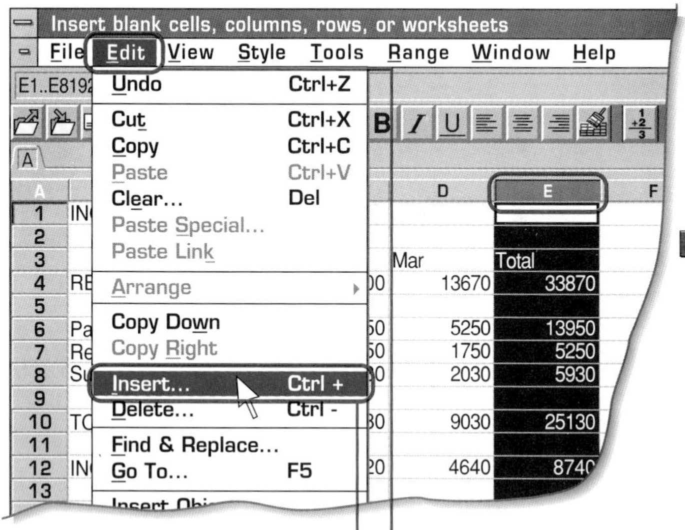

A new column will appear to the left of the column you select.

1 To select a column, move the mouse over the column heading (example: **column E**) and then press the left button.

2 Move the mouse over **Edit** and then press the left button.

3 Move the mouse over **Insert** and then press the left button.

You can
add a column to your
worksheet at any time.
The existing columns
shift to make room
for the new
column.

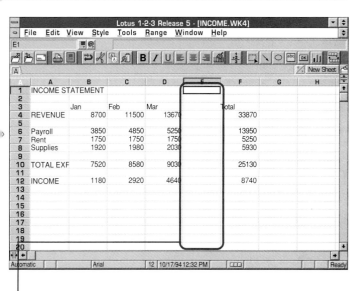

◆ The new column
appears and all the
columns that follow
shift to the right.

DELETE A ROW

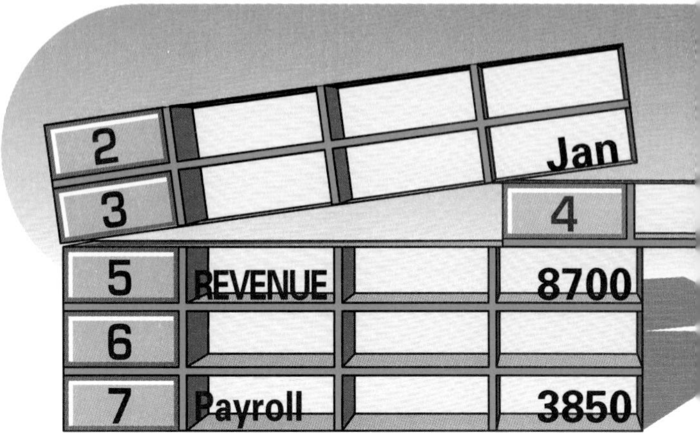

DELETE A ROW

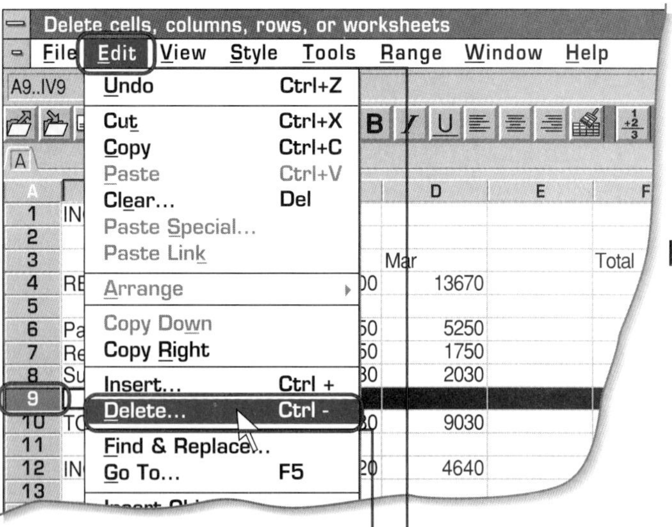

1 To select the row you want to delete, move the mouse over the row heading (example: **row 9**) and then press the left button.

2 Move the mouse over **Edit** and then press the left button.

3 Move the mouse over **Delete** and then press the left button.

You can delete a row from your worksheet. This lets you remove cells you no longer need.

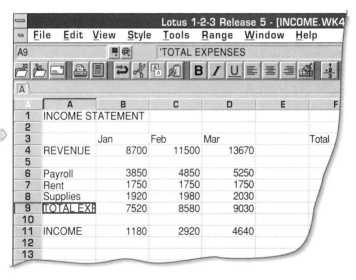

◆ The row disappears and all the rows that follow shift upward.

DELETE A COLUMN

DELETE A COLUMN

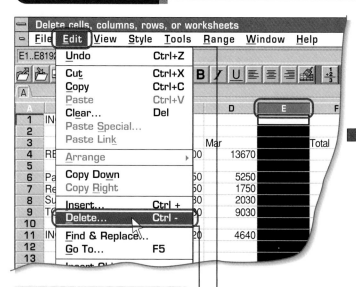

1 To select the column you want to delete, move the mouse ⌖ over the column heading (example: **column E**) and then press the left button.

2 Move the mouse ⌖ over **Edit** and then press the left button.

3 Move the mouse ⌖ over **Delete** and then press the left button.

When you delete a column, the remaining columns move to fill the empty space.

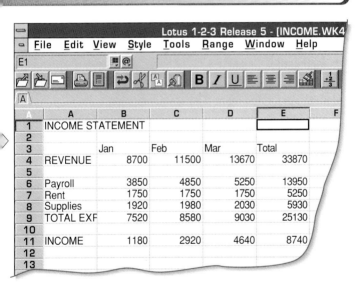

	A	B	C	D	E	F
1	INCOME STATEMENT					
2						
3		Jan	Feb	Mar	Total	
4	REVENUE	8700	11500	13670	33870	
5						
6	Payroll	3850	4850	5250	13950	
7	Rent	1750	1750	1750	5250	
8	Supplies	1920	1980	2030	5930	
9	TOTAL EXF	7520	8580	9030	25130	
10						
11	INCOME	1180	2920	4640	8740	
12						
13						

◆ The column disappears and all the columns that follow shift to the left.

CHANGE COLUMN WIDTH

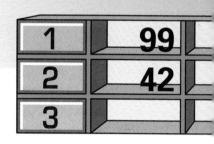

CHANGE COLUMN WIDTH

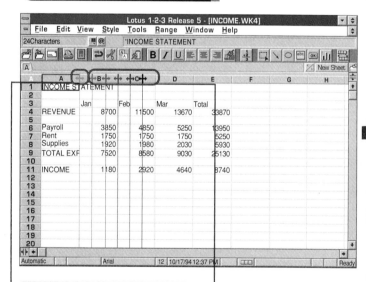

1 Move the mouse ⌖ over the right edge of the column heading you want to change (example: **column A**) and ⌖ changes to ┿ .

2 Press and hold down the left button as you drag the edge of the column to a new position.

◆ A black line indicates the new column width.

126

You can improve the appearance of your worksheet and display hidden data by changing the width of columns.

33 870
678 100
110 567

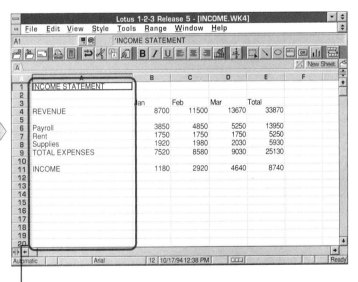

3 Release the button and the new column width appears.

127

CHANGE COLUMN WIDTH

CHANGE COLUMN WIDTH AUTOMATICALLY

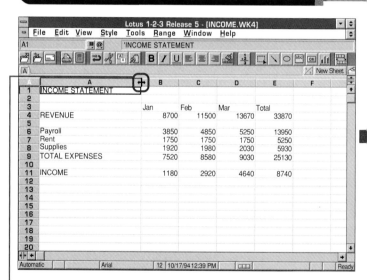

1 Move the mouse ⬚ over the right edge of the column heading you want to change (example: **column A**) and ⬚ changes to **+**.

2 Quickly press the left button twice.

You can have 1-2-3 adjust a column width to fit the longest item in the column.

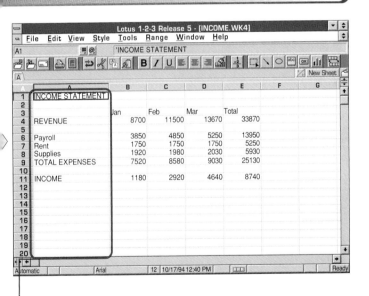

◆ The column width changes to fit the longest item in the column.

CHANGE ROW HEIGHT

CHANGE ROW HEIGHT

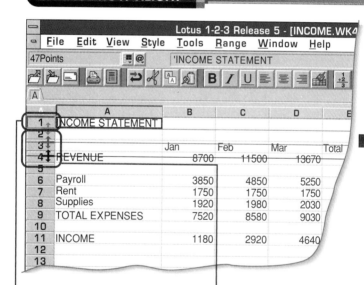

1 Move the mouse ⬚ over the bottom edge of the row heading you want to change (example: **row 1**) and ⬚ changes to ✚.

2 Press and hold down the left button as you drag the edge of the row to a new position.

◆ A black line indicates the new row height.

You can change the height of a row. This is useful if you want to add space between the rows of data in your worksheet.

	Lotus 1-2-3 Release 5 - [INCOME.WK4]

File   Edit   View   Style   Tools   Range   Window   Help

A1   ■ @   'INCOME STATEMENT

	A	B	C	D	E
1	INCOME STATEMENT				
2					
3		Jan	Feb	Mar	Total
4	REVENUE	8700	11500	13670	
5					
6	Payroll	3850	4850	5250	
7	Rent	1750	1750	1750	
8	Supplies	1920	1980	2030	
9	TOTAL EXPENSES	7520	8580	9030	
10					
11	INCOME	1180	2920		

3 Release the button and the new row height appears.

CHANGE ROW HEIGHT

You can have 1-2-3 adjust a row height to fit the tallest item in the row.

CHANGE ROW HEIGHT AUTOMATICALLY

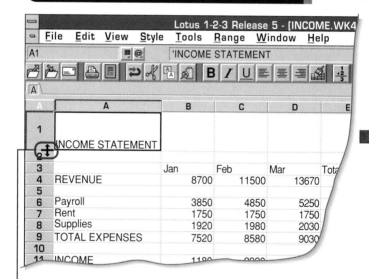

1 Move the mouse ⌖ over the bottom edge of the row heading you want to change (example: **row 1**) and ⌖ changes to ⬍.

2 Quickly press the left button twice.

	Lotus 1-2-3 Release 5 - [INCOME.WK4]				

File Edit View Style Tools Range Window Help

A1   ■@   'INCOME STATEMENT

	A	B	C	D	E
1	INCOME STATEMENT				
2					
3		Jan	Feb	Mar	Total
4	REVENUE	8700	11500	13670	3
5					
6	Payroll	3850	4850	5250	
7	Rent	1750	1750	1750	
8	Supplies	1920	1980	2030	
9	TOTAL EXPENSES	7520	8580	9030	
10					
11	INCOME	1180	2920	4640	
12					
13					

◆ The row height changes
to fit the tallest item in the row.

133

CHANGE APPEARANCE OF NUMBERS

Number Style	Example
Scientific	1.04E+03
Comma	1,038.00
Percent	103800.00%
US Dollar	$1,038.00
Japanese Yen	¥1,038

CHANGE APPEARANCE OF NUMBERS

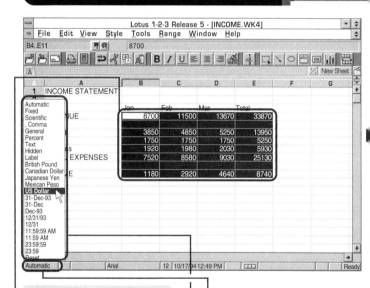

1 Select the cells containing the numbers you want to change.

Note: To select cells, refer to pages 26 to 29.

2 Move the mouse ⫣ over this box and then press the left button.

3 Move the mouse ⫣ over the style you want to use (example: **US Dollar**) and then press the left button.

134

You can change the appearance of numbers in your worksheet without retyping them. This can make the numbers easier to understand.

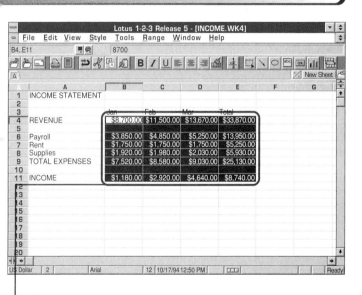

◆ The numbers in the cells you selected display the new style.

*Note: If asterisks (*) appear in a cell, the column is not wide enough to display the entire number. To change the column width, refer to pages 126 to 129.*

CHANGE NUMBER OF DECIMAL PLACES

You can change the number of decimal places displayed in your worksheet.

CHANGE NUMBER OF DECIMAL PLACES

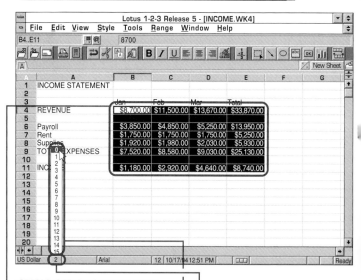

1 Select the cells containing the numbers you want to change.

Note: To select cells, refer to pages 26 to 29.

2 Move the mouse � over this box and then press the left button.

3 Move the mouse � over the number of decimal places you want to display (example: **0**) and then press the left button.

136

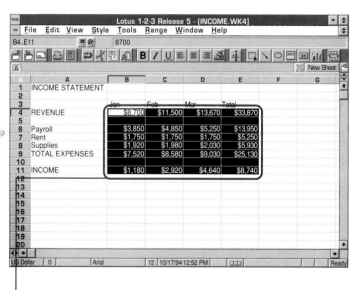

<table>
<tr><td colspan="8">Lotus 1-2-3 Release 5 - [INCOME.WK4]</td></tr>
</table>

File	Edit	View	Style	Tools	Range	Window	Help

B4..E11		8700				

	A	B	C	D	E	F	G
1	INCOME STATEMENT						
2							
3		Jan	Feb	Mar	Total		
4	REVENUE	$8,700	$11,500	$13,670	$33,870		
5							
6	Payroll	$3,850	$4,850	$5,250	$13,950		
7	Rent	$1,750	$1,750	$1,750	$5,250		
8	Supplies	$1,920	$1,980	$2,030	$5,930		
9	TOTAL EXPENSES	$7,520	$8,580	$9,030	$25,130		
10							
11	INCOME	$1,180	$2,920	$4,640	$8,740		
12							
13							
14							
15							
16							
17							
18							
19							
20							

| US Dollar | 0 | | Arial | | 12 | 10/17/94 12:52 PM | | | Ready |

◆ The numbers in
the cells you selected
display the new number
of decimal places.

BOLD, ITALIC AND UNDERLINE

bold   *italic*   <u>underline</u>

BOLD, ITALIC AND UNDERLINE

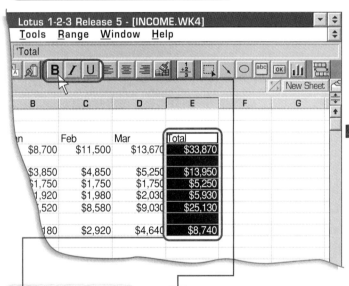

1 Select the cells containing the data you want to change.

Note: To select cells, refer to pages 26 to 29.

2 Move the mouse ⟨⟩ over one of the following options and then press the left button.

B Bold data

I Italicize data

<u>U</u> Underline data

138

You can
use the Bold, Italic
and Underline features
to emphasize important
data.

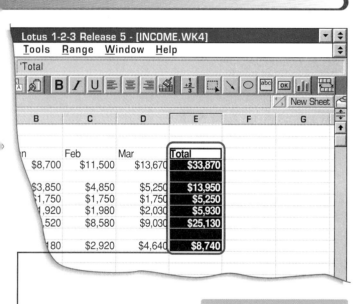

◆ The data in the cells
you selected appears in
the new style.

*Note: In this example, the
data appears in the bold style.*

**Remove Bold, Italic
or Underline**

Repeat steps **1** and **2**.

ALIGN DATA

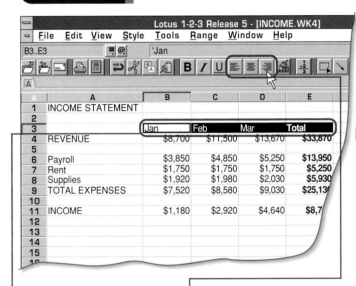

Lotus 1-2-3 Release 5 - [INCOME.WK4]

File   Edit   View   Style   Tools   Range   Window   Help

B3..E3   'Jan

	A	B	C	D	E
1	INCOME STATEMENT				
2					
3		Jan	Feb	Mar	Total
4	REVENUE	$8,700	$11,500	$13,670	$33,870
5					
6	Payroll	$3,850	$4,850	$5,250	$13,950
7	Rent	$1,750	$1,750	$1,750	$5,250
8	Supplies	$1,920	$1,980	$2,030	$5,930
9	TOTAL EXPENSES	$7,520	$8,580	$9,030	$25,13
10					
11	INCOME	$1,180	$2,920	$4,640	$8,7
12					
13					
14					
15					

1 Select the cells containing the data you want to align.

Note: To select cells, refer to pages 26 to 29.

2 Move the mouse ⇧ over one of the following options and then press the left button.

 Left-align data

 Center data

Right-align data

You can change the position of data in each cell of your worksheet. 1-2-3 offers three alignment options.

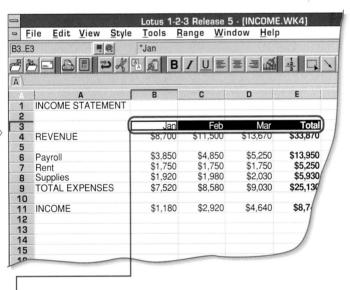

◆ The data in the cells you selected displays the new alignment.

Note: In this example, the data appears right-aligned in the cells.

CHANGE FONTS

CHANGE TYPEFACE

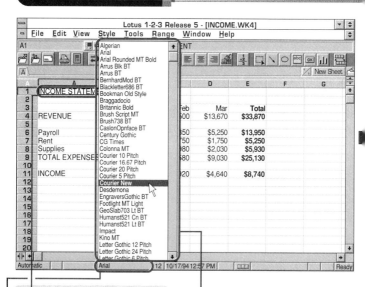

1 Select the cell(s) containing the data you want to change to a new typeface (example: **A1**).

2 Move the mouse ⌖ over this box and then press the left button.

3 Move the mouse ⌖ over the typeface you want to use (example: **Courier New**) and then press the left button.

Note: To view all of the available typefaces, use the scroll bar. For more information, refer to page 40.

You can
change the design
of data to give
your worksheet
a new look.

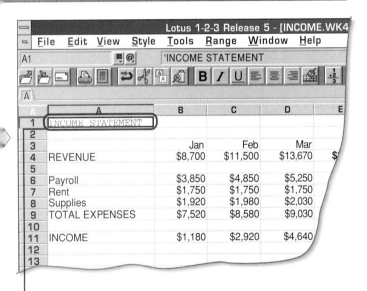

The data in the
cell(s) you selected
changes to the new
typeface.

143

CHANGE FONTS

6 point

12 point

14 point

18 point

24 point

1-2-3 measures the size of data in points. There are approximately 72 points per inch.

CHANGE FONT SIZE

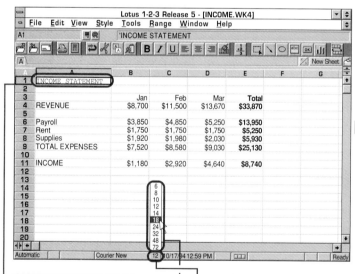

1 Select the cell(s) containing the data you want to change to a new font size.

2 Move the mouse ▷ over this box and then press the left button.

3 Move the mouse ▷ over the font size you want to use (example: **18**) and then press the left button.

You can change the size of data in your worksheet to make the data easier to read.

	Lotus 1-2-3 Release 5 - [INCOME.WK4

File   Edit   View   Style   Tools   Range   Window   Help

A1   🔲 @   'INCOME STATEMENT

B *I* U

	A	B	C	D	E
1	INCOME STATEMENT				
2					
3		Jan	Feb	Mar	
4	REVENUE	$8,700	$11,500	$13,670	$
5					
6	Payroll	$3,850	$4,850	$5,250	
7	Rent	$1,750	$1,750	$1,750	
8	Supplies	$1,920	$1,980	$2,030	
9	TOTAL EXPENSES	$7,520	$8,580	$9,030	
10					
11	INCOME	$1,180	$2,920	$4,640	
12					

◆ The data in the cell(s) you selected changes to the new font size.

145

CHANGE FONTS

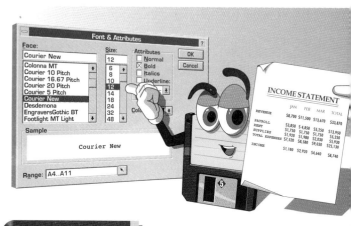

CHANGE FONTS

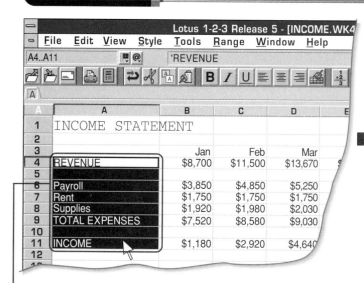

Lotus 1-2-3 Release 5 - [INCOME.WK4

File Edit View Style Tools Range Window Help

A4..A11   'REVENUE

	A	B	C	D	E
1	INCOME STATEMENT				
2					
3		Jan	Feb	Mar	
4	REVENUE	$8,700	$11,500	$13,670	
5					
6	Payroll	$3,850	$4,850	$5,250	
7	Rent	$1,750	$1,750	$1,750	
8	Supplies	$1,920	$1,980	$2,030	
9	TOTAL EXPENSES	$7,520	$8,580	$9,030	
10					
11	INCOME	$1,180	$2,920	$4,640	
12					

1 Select the cells containing the data you want to change.

Note: To select cells, refer to pages 26 to 29.

146

You can change the design and size of data in your worksheet at the same time by using the Font & Attributes feature.

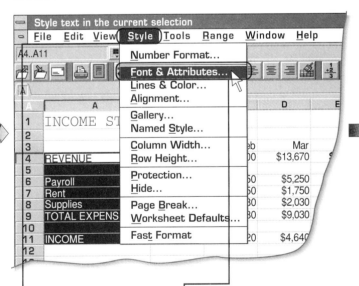

Style text in the current selection						
File	Edit	View	**Style**	Tools	Range	Window	Help

A4..A11

	A				D	E
1	INCOME ST					
2						
3				eb	Mar	
4	REVENUE			00	$13,670	
5						
6	Payroll			50	$5,250	
7	Rent			50	$1,750	
8	Supplies			30	$2,030	
9	TOTAL EXPENS			30	$9,030	
10						
11	INCOME			20	$4,640	
12						

Style menu:
- Number Format...
- **Font & Attributes...**
- Lines & Color...
- Alignment...
- Gallery...
- Named Style...
- Column Width...
- Row Height...
- Protection...
- Hide...
- Page Break...
- Worksheet Defaults...
- Fast Format

2 Move the mouse � over **Style** and then press the left button.

3 Move the mouse � over **Font & Attributes** and then press the left button.

To continue, refer to the next page.

147

CHANGE FONTS

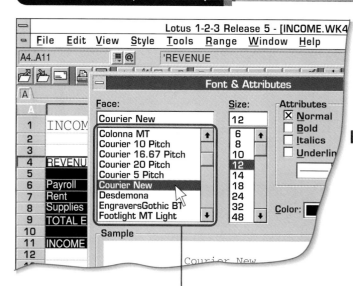

◆ The **Font & Attributes** dialog box appears.

4 Move the mouse ⤵ over the typeface you want to use (example: **Courier New**) and then press the left button.

Note: To view all of the available font options, use the scroll bars. For more information, refer to page 40.

Changing the design and size of data can improve the presentation of your worksheet.

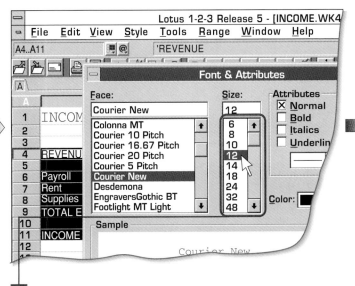

5 Move the mouse ⌖ over the font size you want to use (example: **12**) and then press the left button.

To continue, refer to the next page.

CHANGE FONTS

CHANGE FONTS (CONTINUED)

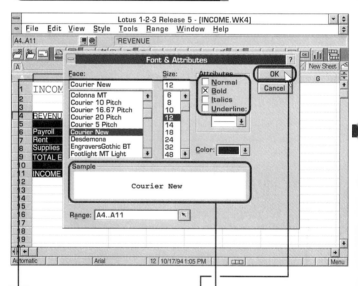

6 Move the mouse ⍉ over an attribute you want to use (example: **Bold**) and then press the left button.

Note: ☒ *indicates an attribute is on.*
☐ *indicates an attribute is off.*

◆ This area displays a sample of the font options you selected.

7 Move the mouse ⍉ ove **OK** and then press the left button.

The Font & Attributes dialog box displays a sample of the font options you selected. This lets you see exactly how the data will appear in your worksheet.

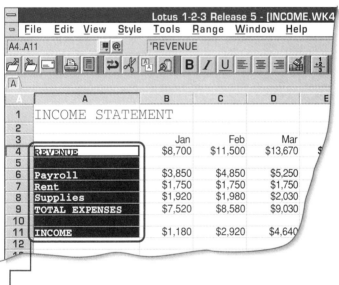

◆ The data in the cells you selected displays the font changes.

151

CENTER DATA ACROSS COLUMNS

You can center data across columns in your worksheet.

CENTER DATA ACROSS COLUMNS

```
                    Lotus 1-2-3 Release 5 - [INCOME.WK4]
  File  Edit  View  Style  Tools  Range  Window  Help
A1..E1              @        'INCOME STATEMENT
```

	A	B	C	D	E
1	INCOME STATEMENT				
2					
3		Jan	Feb	Mar	Total
4	REVENUE	$8,700	$11,500	$13,670	$33,870
5					
6	Payroll	$3,850	$4,850	$5,250	$13,950
7	Rent	$1,750	$1,750	$1,750	$5,250
8	Supplies	$1,920	$1,980	$2,030	$5,930
9	TOTAL EXPENSES	$7,520	$8,580	$9,030	$25,13
10					
11	INCOME	$1,180	$2,920	$4,640	$8,7
12					
13					
14					
15					

1 To center data across columns, select the cells you want to center the data between.

Note: For best results, the first cell you select should contain the data you want to center.

152

Align data in a range or query table						
<u>F</u>ile	<u>E</u>dit	<u>V</u>iew	**Style**	<u>T</u>ools	<u>R</u>ange	<u>W</u>indow <u>H</u>elp

A1..E1   NT

	A			D	E
1	INCOME ST				
2					
3			eb	Mar	
4	**REVENUE**		)0	$13,670	
5					
6	Payroll		50	$5,250	
7	Rent		50	$1,750	
8	Supplies		30	$2,030	
9	TOTAL EXPENS		30	$9,030	
10					
11	INCOME		20	$4,640	
12					

Menu items under Style:
- <u>N</u>umber Format...
- <u>F</u>ont & Attributes...
- <u>L</u>ines & Color...
- <u>A</u>lignment...
- <u>G</u>allery...
- Named <u>S</u>tyle...
- <u>C</u>olumn Width...
- <u>R</u>ow Height...
- <u>P</u>rotection...
- <u>H</u>ide...
- Page <u>B</u>reak...
- <u>W</u>orksheet Defaults...
- Fas<u>t</u> Format

2 Move the mouse ⌖ over **Style** and then press the left button.

3 Move the mouse ⌖ over **Alignment** and then press the left button.

To continue, refer to the next page.

153

CENTER DATA ACROSS COLUMNS

Centering data across columns is useful for displaying titles in your worksheet.

CENTER DATA ACROSS COLUMNS (CONTINUED)

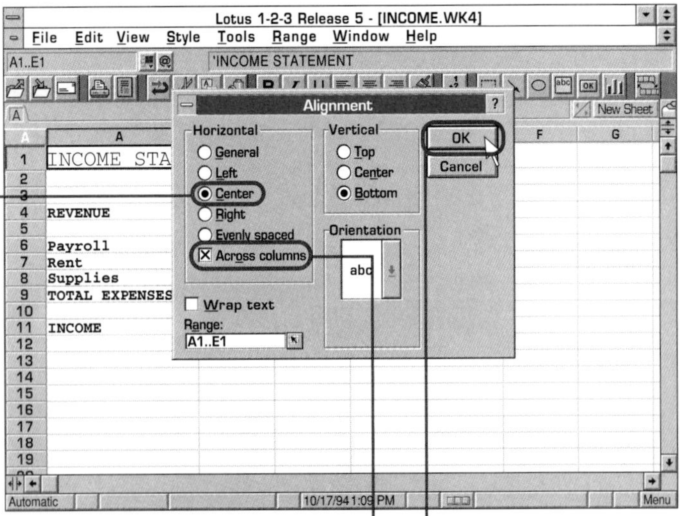

◆ The **Alignment** dialog box appears.

4 To center the data across columns, move the mouse ⇖ over **Center** and then press the left button (O changes to ◉).

5 Move the mouse ⇖ over **Across columns** and then press the left button (☐ changes to ☒).

6 Move the mouse ⇖ over **OK** and then press the left button.

	Lotus 1-2-3 Release 5 - [INCOME.WK4]			
File Edit View Style Tools Range Window Help				

A1..E1   ^INCOME STATEMENT

	A	B	C	D	E
1	INCOME STATEMENT				
2					
3		Jan	Feb	Mar	Total
4	REVENUE	$8,700	$11,500	$13,670	$33,870
5					
6	Payroll	$3,850	$4,850	$5,250	$13,950
7	Rent	$1,750	$1,750	$1,750	$5,250
8	Supplies	$1,920	$1,980	$2,030	$5,930
9	TOTAL EXPENSES	$7,520	$8,580	$9,030	$25,13
10					
11	INCOME	$1,180	$2,920	$4,640	$8,7
12					
13					
14					
15					

◆ The data appears
centered between the
cells you selected.

155

ADD BORDERS

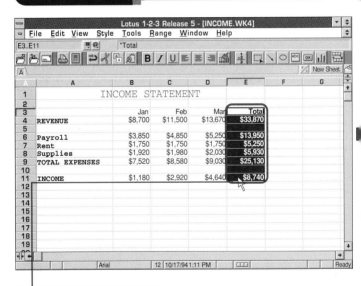

1 Select the cells you want to display borders.

Note: To select cells, refer to pages 26 to 29.

You can add borders to draw attention to important data in your worksheet.

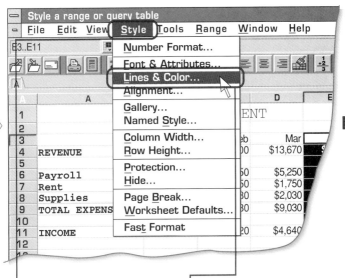

Style a range or query table

File   Edit   View   **Style**   Tools   Range   Window   Help

B3..E11

Number Format...
Font & Attributes...
Lines & Color...
Alignment...

Gallery...
Named Style...

Column Width...
Row Height...

Protection...
Hide...

Page Break...
Worksheet Defaults...

Fast Format

	A		D	E
1		ENT		
2				
3			eb	Mar
4	REVENUE		00	$13,670
5				
6	Payroll		50	$5,250
7	Rent		50	$1,750
8	Supplies		30	$2,030
9	TOTAL EXPENS		30	$9,030
10				
11	INCOME		20	$4,640
12				

2 Move the mouse ⌖ over **Style** and then press the left button.

3 Move the mouse ⌖ over **Lines & Color** and then press the left button.

To continue, refer to the next page.

157

ADD BORDERS

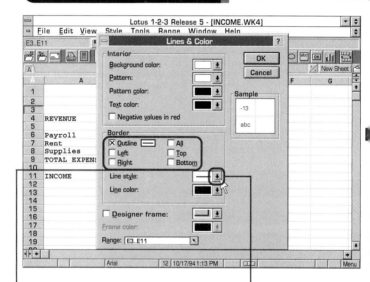

◆ The **Lines & Color** dialog box appears.

4 Move the mouse ⓀＲ over the border you want to add (example: **Outline**) and then press the left button. □ changes to ⊠.

5 To select a line style for the border, move the mouse ⓀＲ over ⬇ and then press the left button.

1-2-3
offers a variety
of line styles that
you can choose
from.

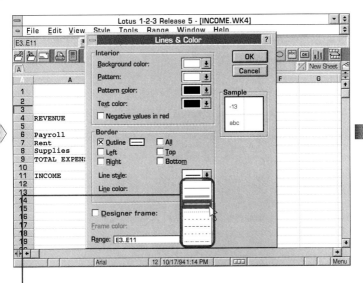

6 Move the mouse ⌖ over the line style you want to use and then press the left button.

7 Repeat steps **4** to **6** for each border you want to add.

To continue, refer to the next page.

159

ADD BORDERS

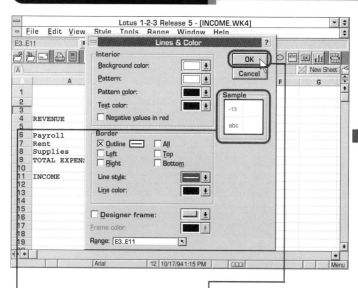

◆ This area displays
a sample of the border(s)
you selected.

8 Move the mouse ⌖
over **OK** and then press
the left button.

The Lines & Color
dialog box displays a
sample of the borders
you selected. This lets
you see exactly how the
borders will appear in
your worksheet.

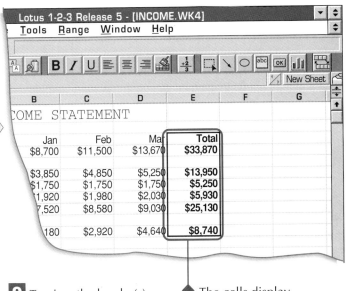

	B	C	D	E	F	G
			Ma	**Total**		
	Jan	Feb				
	$8,700	$11,500	$13,670	**$33,870**		
	$3,850	$4,850	$5,250	**$13,950**		
	$1,750	$1,750	$1,750	**$5,250**		
	1,920	$1,980	$2,030	**$5,930**		
	7,520	$8,580	$9,030	**$25,130**		
	180	$2,920	$4,640	**$8,740**		

COME STATEMENT

Lotus 1-2-3 Release 5 - [INCOME.WK4]
Tools   Range   Window   Help

New Sheet

9 To view the border(s),
move the mouse ⋈ outside
the selected area and then
press the left button.

◆ The cells display
the border(s).

161

STYLE DATA AUTOMATICALLY

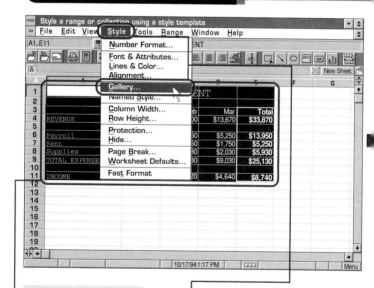

Style a range or collection using a style template

| File | Edit | View | Style | Tools | Range | Window | Help |

A1..E11

Number Format...
Font & Attributes...
Lines & Color...
Alignment...
Gallery...
Named Style...
Column Width...
Row Height...
Protection...
Hide...
Page Break...
Worksheet Defaults...
Fast Format

10/17/94 1:17 PM   Menu

1 Select the cells containing the data you want to style.

Note: To select cells, refer to pages 26 to 29.

2 Move the mouse ⬡ over **Style** and then press the left button.

3 Move the mouse ⬡ over **Gallery** and then press the left button.

162

You can use
the Gallery feature to
quickly change the overall
appearance of data in
your worksheet.

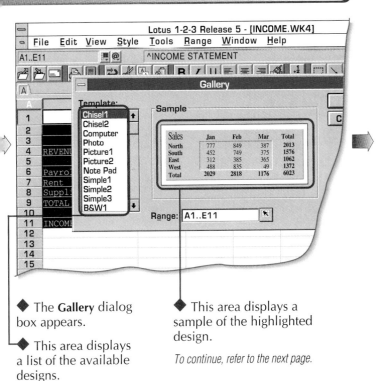

◆ The **Gallery** dialog
box appears.

◆ This area displays
a list of the available
designs.

◆ This area displays a
sample of the highlighted
design.

To continue, refer to the next page.

163

STYLE DATA AUTOMATICALLY

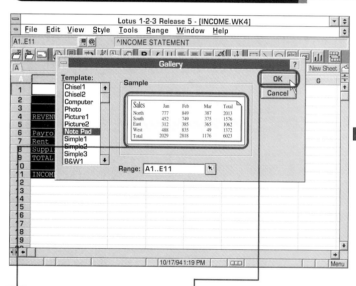

4 Press ↓ or ↑ on your keyboard until the **Sample** box displays the design you want to use (example: **Note Pad**).

5 To select the highlighted design, move the mouse ⇱ over **OK** and then press the left button.

You can select from fourteen different designs to give your worksheet a more polished and professional look.

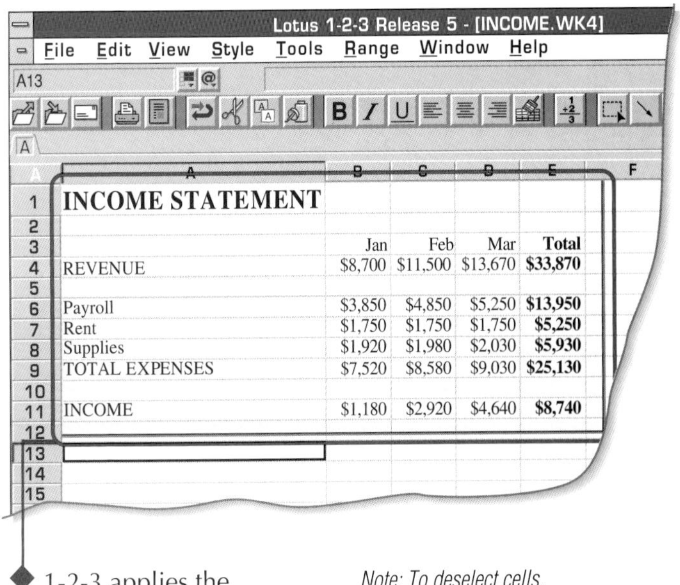

◆ 1-2-3 applies the design to the cells you selected.

Note: To deselect cells, move the mouse outside the selected area and then press the left button.

PREVIEW A WORKSHEET

PREVIEW A WORKSHEET

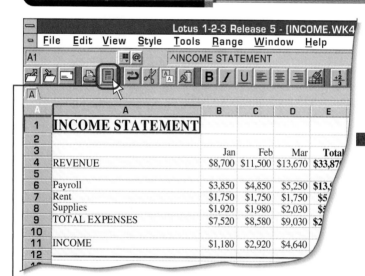

```
                    Lotus 1-2-3 Release 5 - [INCOME.WK4
  File   Edit   View   Style   Tools   Range   Window   Help
A1              @        ^INCOME STATEMENT
```

	A	B	C	D	E
1	**INCOME STATEMENT**				
2					
3		Jan	Feb	Mar	**Total**
4	REVENUE	$8,700	$11,500	$13,670	**$33,87**
5					
6	Payroll	$3,850	$4,850	$5,250	**$13,9**
7	Rent	$1,750	$1,750	$1,750	**$5,**
8	Supplies	$1,920	$1,980	$2,030	**$5**
9	TOTAL EXPENSES	$7,520	$8,580	$9,030	**$2**
10					
11	INCOME	$1,180	$2,920	$4,640	
12					

1 To preview the worksheet displayed on your screen, move the mouse ⌖ over 🖩 and then press the left button.

◆ The **Print Preview** dialog box appears.

The Print Preview feature lets you see on screen how your worksheet will look when printed.

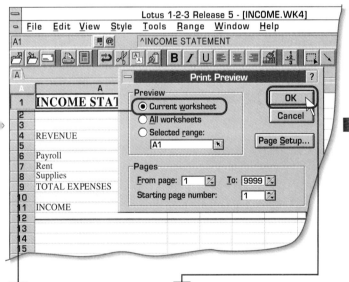

2 Move the mouse ⤵ over **Current worksheet** and then press the left button (○ changes to ◉).

3 Move the mouse ⤵ over **OK** and then press the left button.

To continue, refer to the next page.

167

PREVIEW A WORKSHEET

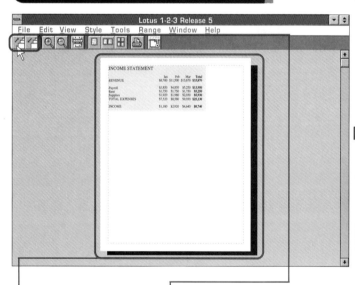

◆ Your worksheet appears in the Print Preview window.

4 To view the next page, move the mouse ⬡ over ⬚ and then press the left button.

◆ To view the previous page, move the mouse ⬡ over ⬚ and then press the left button.

168

If your worksheet consists of more than one page, you can use these SmartIcons to switch between the pages in the Print Preview window.

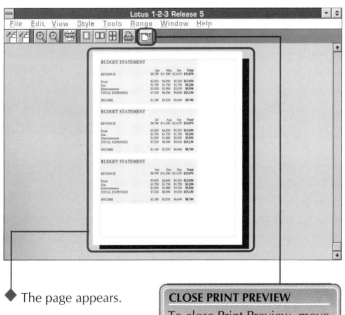

◆ The page appears.

Note: In this example, the worksheet contains more than one page.

CLOSE PRINT PREVIEW

To close Print Preview, move the mouse ⬍ over 🖾 and then press the left button.

PREVIEW A WORKSHEET

MAGNIFY A PAGE

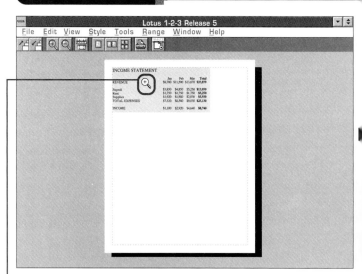

1 To magnify an area of the page, move the mouse ⊕ over the area and then press the left button.

Note: To display your worksheet in the Print Preview window, refer to page 166.

In Print Preview, you can magnify a page to enlarge the display of data.

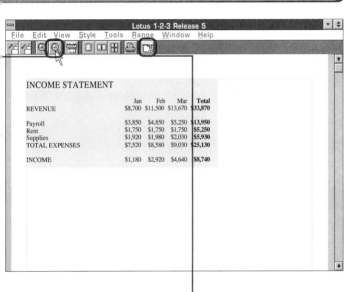

INCOME STATEMENT

	Jan	Feb	Mar	Total
REVENUE	$8,700	$11,500	$13,670	$33,870
Payroll	$3,850	$4,850	$5,250	$13,950
Rent	$1,750	$1,750	$1,750	$5,250
Supplies	$1,920	$1,980	$2,030	$5,930
TOTAL EXPENSES	$7,520	$8,580	$9,030	$25,130
INCOME	$1,180	$2,920	$4,640	$8,740

◆ A magnified view of the area appears.

2 To reduce the display of the area, move the mouse ⟍ over 🔍 and then press the left button.

CLOSE PRINT PREVIEW

To close Print Preview, move the mouse ⟍ over 🔲 and then press the left button.

171

PRINT A WORKSHEET

PRINT A WORKSHEET

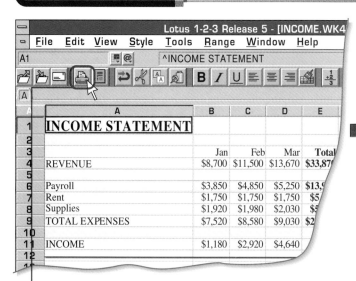

Lotus 1-2-3 Release 5 - [INCOME.WK4

| File | Edit | View | Style | Tools | Range | Window | Help |

A1   ^INCOME STATEMENT

	A	B	C	D	E
1	**INCOME STATEMENT**				
2					
3		Jan	Feb	Mar	**Total**
4	REVENUE	$8,700	$11,500	$13,670	**$33,87**
5					
6	Payroll	$3,850	$4,850	$5,250	**$13,9**
7	Rent	$1,750	$1,750	$1,750	**$5**
8	Supplies	$1,920	$1,980	$2,030	**$5**
9	TOTAL EXPENSES	$7,520	$8,580	$9,030	**$2**
10					
11	INCOME	$1,180	$2,920	$4,640	
12					

1 To print the worksheet displayed on your screen, move the mouse ⬐ over 🖨 and then press the left button.

◆ The **Print** dialog box appears.

You can print the worksheet displayed on your screen. Before printing, make sure your printer is on and it contains paper.

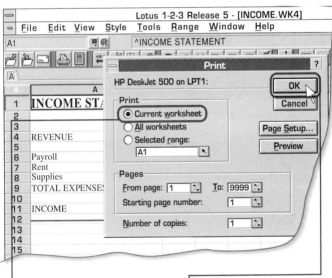

2 Move the mouse ⌖ over **Current worksheet** and then press the left button (○ changes to ●).

3 Move the mouse ⌖ over **OK** and then press the left button.

173

ADD A PAGE BREAK

If you want to start a new page at a specific place in your worksheet, you can add a page break.

ADD A PAGE BREAK

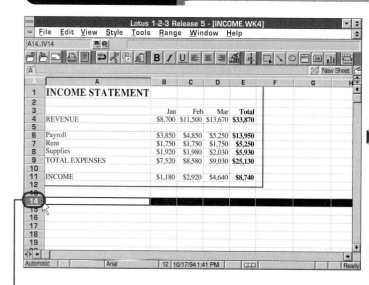

	Lotus 1-2-3 Release 5 - [INCOME.WK4]						▼ ◆
File Edit View Style Tools Range Window Help							◆

A14..IV14

	A	B	C	D	E	F	G	H
1	**INCOME STATEMENT**							
2								
3		Jan	Feb	Mar	Total			
4	REVENUE	$8,700	$11,500	$13,670	**$33,870**			
5								
6	Payroll	$3,850	$4,850	$5,250	**$13,950**			
7	Rent	$1,750	$1,750	$1,750	**$5,250**			
8	Supplies	$1,920	$1,980	$2,030	**$5,930**			
9	TOTAL EXPENSES	$7,520	$8,580	$9,030	**$25,130**			
10								
11	INCOME	$1,180	$2,920	$4,640	**$8,740**			
12								
13								
14								
15								
16								
17								
18								
19								

Automatic — Arial — 12 — 10/17/94 1:41 PM — Ready

Across a Page

1-2-3 adds a page break above the row you select.

1 To select a row, move the mouse ⫶ over the row heading and then press the left button.

Down a Page

1-2-3 adds a page break to the left of the column you select.

◆ To select a column, move the mouse ⫶ over the column heading and then press the left button.

174

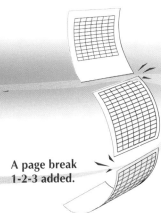

A page break you added.

A page break 1-2-3 added.

If the data in your worksheet cannot fit on one page, 1-2-3 automatically starts a new page by adding a page break.

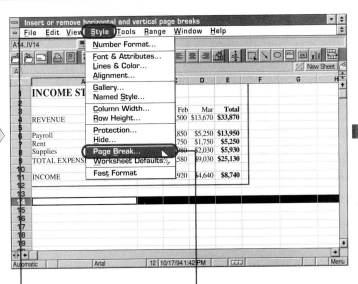

2 Move the mouse ⌖ over **Style** and then press the left button.

3 Move the mouse ⌖ over **Page Break** and then press the left button.

◆ The **Page Break** dialog box appears.

To continue, refer to the next page.

175

ADD A PAGE BREAK

A page break defines where one page ends and another begins.

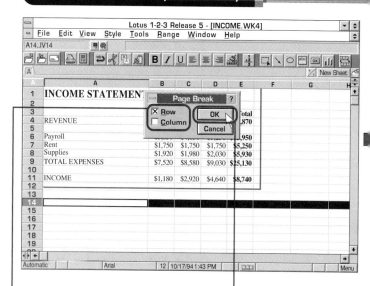

4 To add a page break across the page, move the mouse ⬚ over **Row** and then press the left button (□ changes to ⊠).

◆ To add a page break down the page, move the mouse ⬚ over **Column** and then press the left button.

5 Move the mouse ⬚ over **OK** and then press the left button.

REMOVE A PAGE BREAK

1 To remove a page break, move the mouse ₭ over any cell directly below or directly to the right of the page break line and then press the left button.

2 Perform steps **2** to **5** starting on page 175.

*Note: ⊠ changes to ☐ in step **4**.*

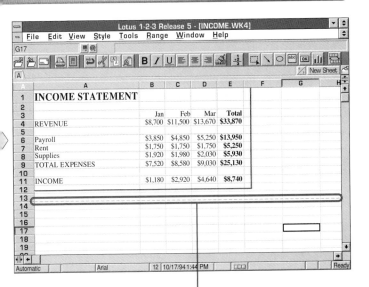

6 To view the page break, move the mouse ₭ over any cell in your worksheet and then press the left button.

◆ A dashed line appears on your screen. This line defines where one page ends and another begins.

Note: This line will not appear when you print your worksheet.

CHANGE PAGE ORIENTATION

If your worksheet is too wide to fit on a page, you can use the Landscape orientation to display more data.

CHANGE PAGE ORIENTATION

Set printed page layout; name and use page settings

File Edit View Style Tools Range Window Help

New	
Open...	Ctrl+O
Close	
Save	Ctrl+S
Save As...	
Doc Info...	
Protect...	
Send Mail...	
Print Preview...	
Page Setup...	
Print...	Ctrl+P
Printer Setup...	
Exit	
1 INCOME.WK4	

	B	C	D	E
:NT				
	Jan	Feb	Mar	**Total**
	$8,700	$11,500	$13,670	**$33,87**
	$3,850	$4,850	$5,250	**$13,**
	$1,750	$1,750	$1,750	**$5**
	$1,920	$1,980	$2,030	**$**
	$7,520	$8,580	$9,030	**$2**
	$1,180	$2,920	$4,640	

1 Move the mouse ⬉ over **File** and then press the left button.

2 Move the mouse ⬉ over **Page Setup** and then press the left button.

◆ The **Page Setup** dialog box appears.

178

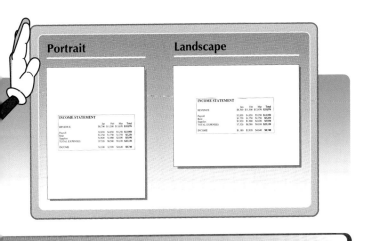

Portrait

Landscape

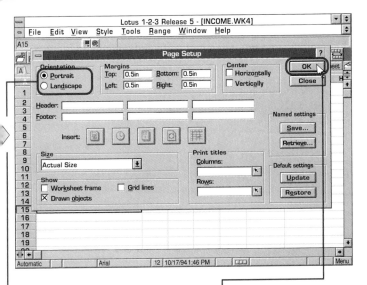

3 Move the mouse ⬚ over the orientation you want to use and then press the left button (○ changes to ⦿).

4 Move the mouse ⬚ over **OK** and then press the left button.

179

CHANGE MARGINS

CHANGE MARGINS

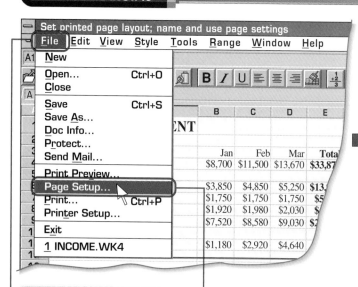

1 Move the mouse over **File** and then press the left button.

2 Move the mouse over **Page Setup** and then press the left button.

A margin is the amount of space between data and the edges of your paper. You can use the Page Setup feature to change the margins.

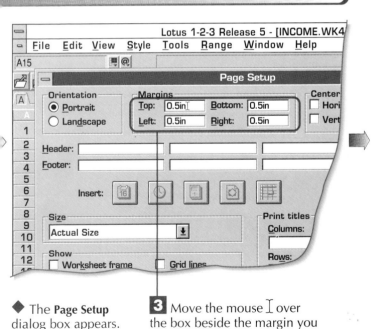

◆ The **Page Setup** dialog box appears.

3 Move the mouse I over the box beside the margin you want to change (example: **Top**) and then press the left button.

To continue, refer to the next page.

181

CHANGE MARGINS

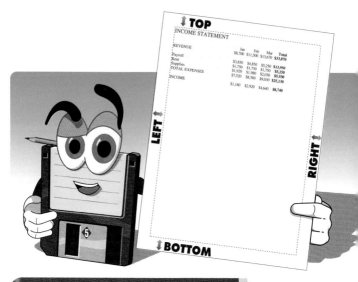

CHANGE MARGINS (CONTINUED)

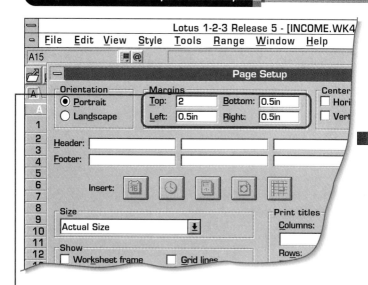

4 Press **←Backspace** or **Delete** to remove the existing margin.

5 Type a new margin in inches (example: **2**).

◆ Repeat steps **3** to **5** starting on page 181 for each margin you want to change.

When you begin a worksheet, the top, bottom, left and right margins are all set at 0.5 inches.

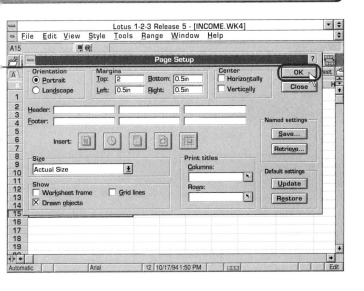

6 Move the mouse ▷ over **OK** and then press the left button.

CHANGE PRINTED DATA SIZE

Set printed page layout; name and use page settings

| File | Edit | View | Style | Tools | Range | Window | Help |

New
Open... Ctrl+O
Close
Save Ctrl+S
Save As...
Doc Info...
Protect...
Send Mail...
Print Preview...
Page Setup...
Print... Ctrl+P
Printer Setup...
Exit
1 INCOME.WK4

	B	C	D	E
NT				
	Jan	Feb	Mar	Total
	$8,700	$11,500	$13,670	$33,87
	$3,850	$4,850	$5,250	$13,
	$1,750	$1,750	$1,750	$5
	$1,920	$1,980	$2,030	$
	$7,520	$8,580	$9,030	$2
	$1,180	$2,920	$4,640	

1 Move the mouse ⬚ over **File** and then press the left button.

2 Move the mouse ⬚ over **Page Setup** and then press the left button.

You can change the size of data on a printed page.

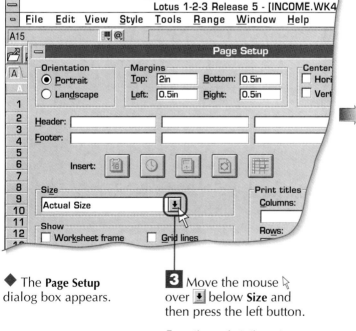

◆ The **Page Setup** dialog box appears.

3 Move the mouse ⬚ over ⬇ below **Size** and then press the left button.

To continue, refer to the next page.

185

CHANGE PRINTED DATA SIZE

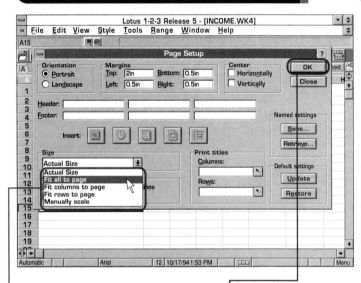

◆ A list of size options appears.

4 Move the mouse ⬚ over the size option you want to use (example: **Fit all to page**) and then press the left button.

5 Move the mouse ⬚ over **OK** and then press the left button.

186

This feature is useful when you want to fit your data on a specific number of pages.

DATA SIZE OPTIONS

Actual Size
Prints the worksheet without increasing or decreasing the data size.

Fit all to page
Decreases the size of data to print the entire worksheet on one page.

Fit columns to page
Decreases the size of data to print all the columns in the worksheet on one page.

Fit rows to page
Decreases the size of data to print all the rows in the worksheet on one page.

ZOOM IN OR OUT

ZOOM IN OR OUT

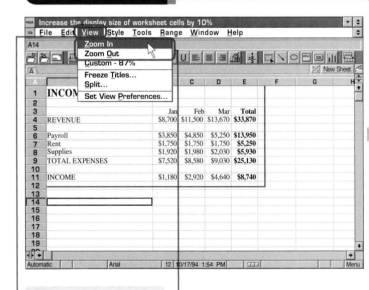

1 Move the mouse ⌖ over **View** and then press the left button.

2 To magnify your worksheet, move the mouse ⌖ over **Zoom In** and then press the left button.

◆ To reduce your worksheet, move the mouse ⌖ over **Zoom Out** and then press the left button.

> You can magnify a worksheet to read small data or reduce a worksheet to view more of your data.

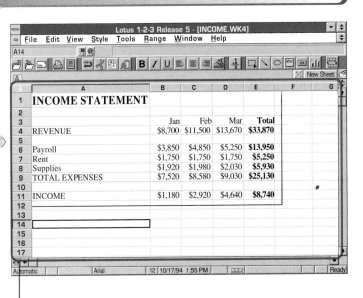

◆ Your worksheet is magnified or reduced by 10%.

◆ To further magnify or reduce your worksheet, repeat steps **1** and **2**.

*Note: To return to the original zoom setting, perform steps **1** and **2**, selecting **Custom - 87%** in step **2**.*

DISPLAY DIFFERENT SMARTICONS

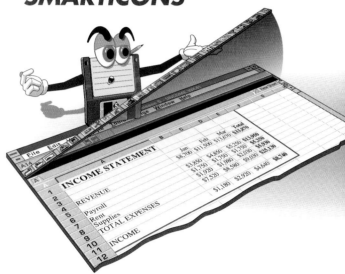

DISPLAY DIFFERENT SMARTICONS

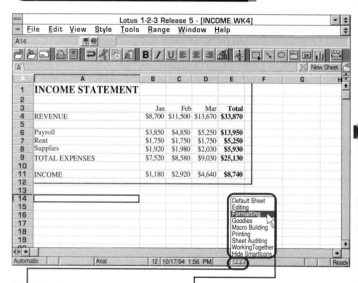

1 To display a list of SmartIcon sets, move the mouse ⍓ over ▦ and then press the left button.

2 Move the mouse ⍓ over the SmartIcon set you want to display (example: **Formatting**) and then press the left button.

SmartIcons let you quickly select commonly used commands. 1-2-3 offers eight sets of SmartIcons, each related to a specific task.

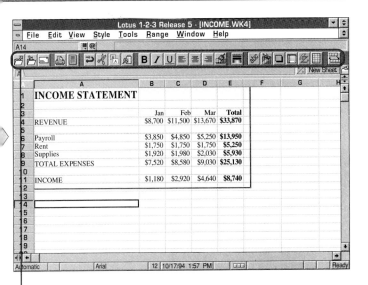

◆ The SmartIcon set you selected appears.

*Note: To return to the original SmartIcon set, repeat steps **1** and **2**, selecting **Default Sheet** in step **2**.*

191

INSERT A WORKSHEET

INSERT A WORKSHEET

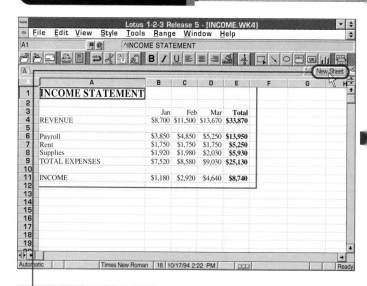

1 Move the mouse ⟋ over **New Sheet** and then press the left button.

A file is like a three-ring binder that contains many sheets. You can add worksheets at any time to store new information.

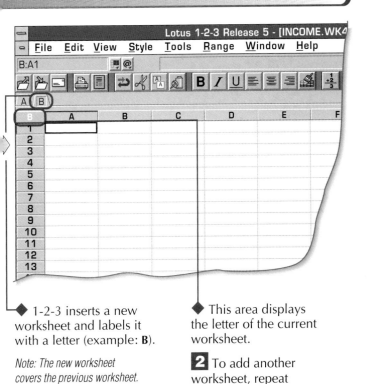

Lotus 1-2-3 Release 5 - [INCOME.WK4

File   Edit   View   Style   Tools   Range   Window   Help

B:A1

A B

B | A | B | C | D | E | F

◆ 1-2-3 inserts a new worksheet and labels it with a letter (example: **B**).

Note: The new worksheet covers the previous worksheet.

◆ This area displays the letter of the current worksheet.

2 To add another worksheet, repeat step **1**.

SWITCH BETWEEN WORKSHEETS

SWITCH BETWEEN WORKSHEETS

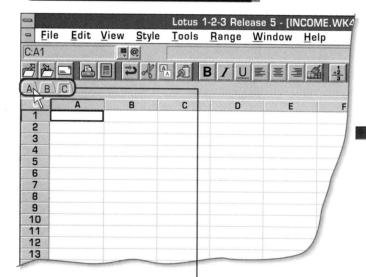

◆ The contents of the current worksheet are displayed on your screen. The contents of the other worksheets are hidden behind this worksheet.

1 To display the contents of another worksheet, move the mouse ⬡ over the worksheet tab (example: **A**) and then press the left button.

> You can easily switch between all of the worksheets in a file. This lets you view the contents of each worksheet.

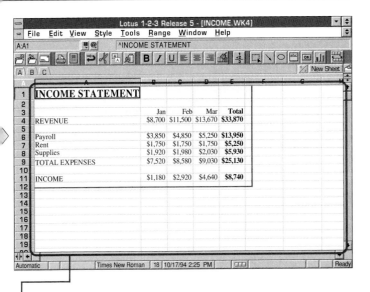

◆ The contents of the worksheet appear.

195

NAME A WORKSHEET

NAME A WORKSHEET

	A	B	C	D	E
1	**INCOME STATEMENT**				
2					
3		Jan	Feb	Mar	**Total**
4	REVENUE	$8,700	$11,500	$13,670	**$33,87**
5					
6	Payroll	$3,850	$4,850	$5,250	**$13,9**
7	Rent	$1,750	$1,750	$1,750	**$5**
8	Supplies	$1,920	$1,980	$2,030	**$5**
9	TOTAL EXPENSES	$7,520	$8,580	$9,030	**$2**
10					
11	INCOME	$1,180	$2,920	$4,640	
12					

Lotus 1-2-3 Release 5 - [INCOME.WK4

File   Edit   View   Style   Tools   Range   Window   Help

A:A1   ^INCOME STATEMENT

1 To name a worksheet, move the mouse ᐟ over the worksheet tab and then quickly press the left button twice.

196

> You can give each worksheet in a file a descriptive name. This helps you remember where you stored your data.

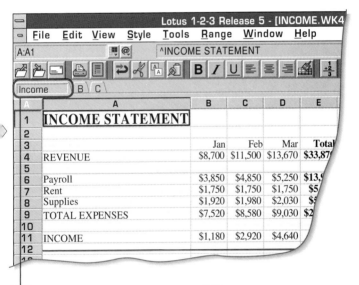

2 Type a name for the worksheet (example: **Income**).

3 Press **Enter** on your keyboard.

VIEW MULTIPLE WORKSHEETS

VIEW MULTIPLE WORKSHEETS

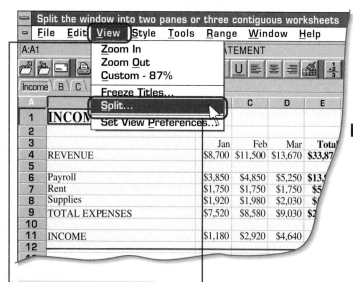

1 Move the mouse ▷ over **View** and then press the left button.

2 Move the mouse ▷ over **Split** and then press the left button.

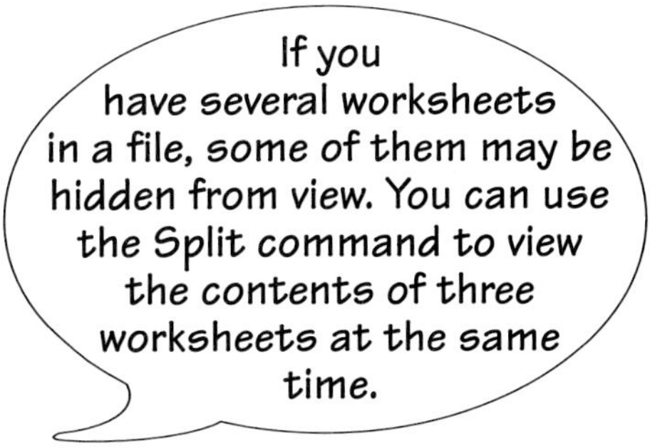
If you have several worksheets in a file, some of them may be hidden from view. You can use the Split command to view the contents of three worksheets at the same time.

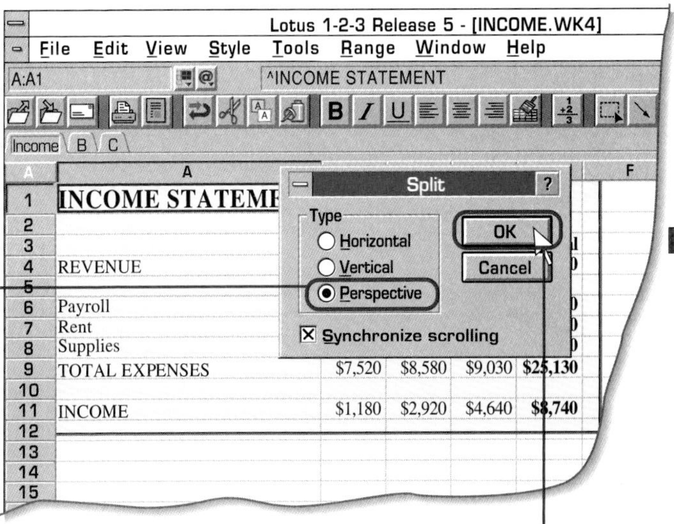
Lotus 1-2-3 Release 5 - [INCOME.WK4]
File Edit View Style Tools Range Window Help
A:A1
^INCOME STATEMENT
Income B C
INCOME STATEMENT
REVENUE
Payroll
Rent
Supplies
TOTAL EXPENSES
$7,520 $8,580 $9,030 $25,130
INCOME
$1,180 $2,920 $4,640 $8,740
Split
Type
Horizontal
Vertical
Perspective
OK
Cancel
Synchronize scrolling

◆ The **Split** dialog box appears.

3 Move the mouse ↖ over **Perspective** and then press the left button (○ changes to ◉).

4 Move the mouse ↖ over **OK** and then press the left button.

To continue, refer to the next page.

VIEW MULTIPLE WORKSHEETS

If your file contains more than three worksheets, you can use your keyboard to display the other worksheets.

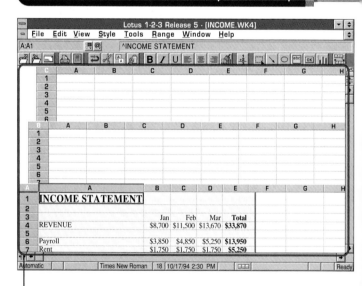

◆ You can now view the contents of your worksheets.

◆ To display the next worksheet in the file, press Ctrl + PageUp.

◆ To display the previous worksheet in the file, press Ctrl + PageDown.

VIEW ONE WORKSHEET

1 Move the mouse ↕ over the worksheet you want to display and then press the left button. 1-2-3 will hide all other worksheets behind this worksheet.

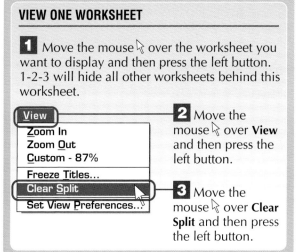

View
- Zoom In
- Zoom Out
- Custom - 87%
- Freeze Titles...
- Clear Split
- Set View Preferences...

2 Move the mouse ↕ over **View** and then press the left button.

3 Move the mouse ↕ over **Clear Split** and then press the left button.

COPY OR MOVE DATA BETWEEN WORKSHEETS

Copying or moving data between worksheets saves you time when you are working in one worksheet and want to use data from another.

COPY OR MOVE DATA BETWEEN WORKSHEETS

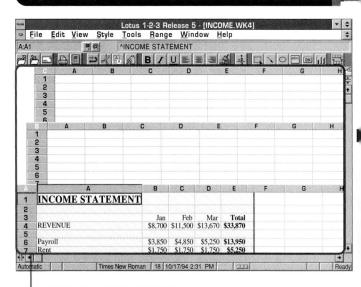

1 Display the worksheets you want to copy or move data between.

Note: To display multiple worksheets, refer to page 198.

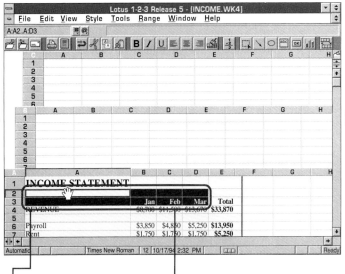

	A	B	C	D	E	F	G	H
1	INCOME STATEMENT							
2								
3			Jan	Feb	Mar	Total		
4	REVENUE		$8,700	$11,500	$13,670	$33,870		
5								
6	Payroll		$3,850	$4,850	$5,250	$13,950		
7	Rent		$1,750	$1,750	$1,750	$5,250		

2 Select the cells you want to copy or move to another worksheet.

Note: To select cells, refer to pages 26 to 29.

3 Move the mouse ⤺ over a border of the cells you selected and ⤺ changes to ✋.

To continue, refer to the next page.

COPY OR MOVE DATA BETWEEN WORKSHEETS

The Copy and Move features both place data in a new location, but they have one distinct difference.

COPY OR MOVE DATA (CONTINUED)

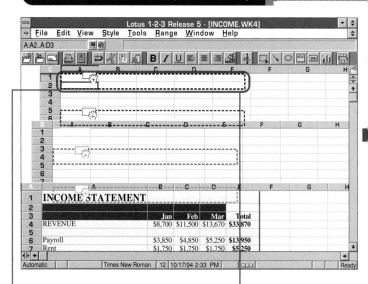

4 To copy the data, press and hold down **Ctrl** and press and hold down the left button as you drag the mouse where you want to place the data.

◆ To move the data, press and hold down the left button as you drag the mouse where you want to place the data.

COPY DATA

When you copy data, the original data remains in its place.

MOVE DATA

When you move data, the original data disappears.

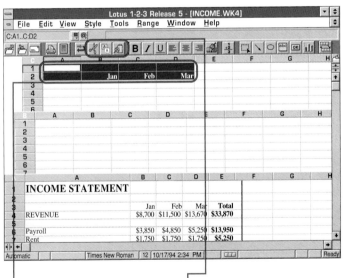

5 Release the left button (and `Ctrl`) and the data appears in the new location.

◆ You can also use these SmartIcons to copy or move data between worksheets. For more information, refer to pages 76 and 80.

CREATE A NEW FILE

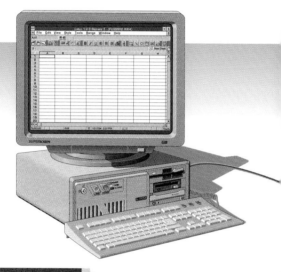

CREATE A NEW FILE

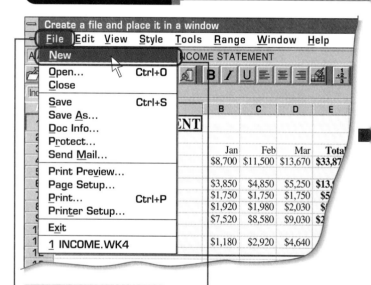

Create a file and place it in a window

| File | Edit | View | Style | Tools | Range | Window | Help |

New

Open...   Ctrl+O
Close

Save   Ctrl+S
Save As...
Doc Info...
Protect...
Send Mail...

Print Preview...
Page Setup...
Print...   Ctrl+P
Printer Setup...

Exit

1 INCOME.WK4

INCOME STATEMENT

B *I* U

	B	C	D	E
	Jan	Feb	Mar	Total
	$8,700	$11,500	$13,670	$33,87
	$3,850	$4,850	$5,250	$13,
	$1,750	$1,750	$1,750	$5
	$1,920	$1,980	$2,030	$
	$7,520	$8,580	$9,030	$2
	$1,180	$2,920	$4,640	

1 Move the mouse ⬡ over **File** and then press the left button.

2 Move the mouse ⬡ over **New** and then press the left button.

You can create a new file to store data on a different topic.

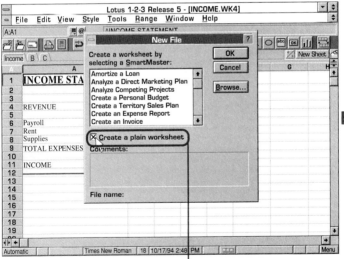

◆ The **New File** dialog box appears.

3 To create a new file, move the mouse ⓡ over this option and then press the left button (☐ changes to ☒).

To continue, refer to the next page.

CREATE A NEW FILE

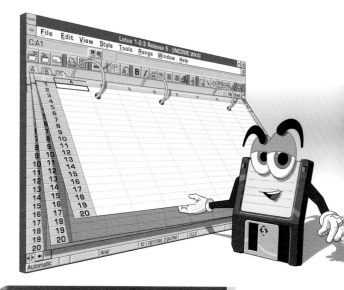

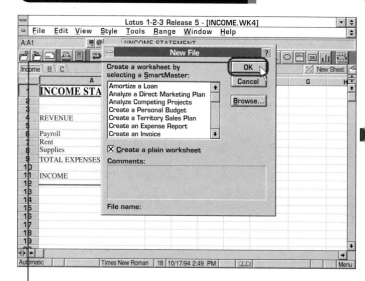

4 Move the mouse ⟋ over **OK** and then press the left button.

Think of each new file as a 3-ring binder. A file can contain multiple worksheets. You can use these worksheets to store related data.

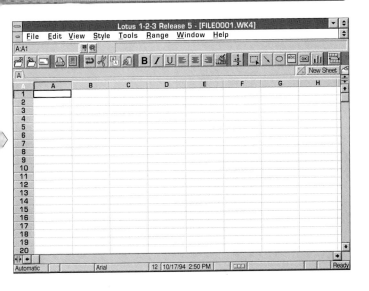

◆ A new file appears.

Note: The previous file is now hidden behind the new file.

SWITCH BETWEEN FILES

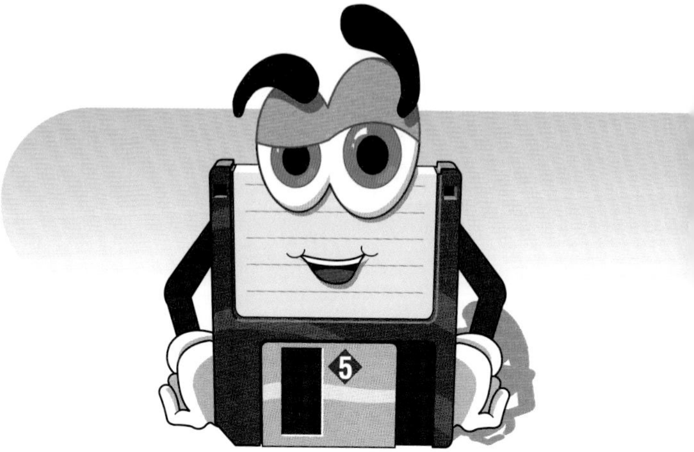

SWITCH BETWEEN FILES

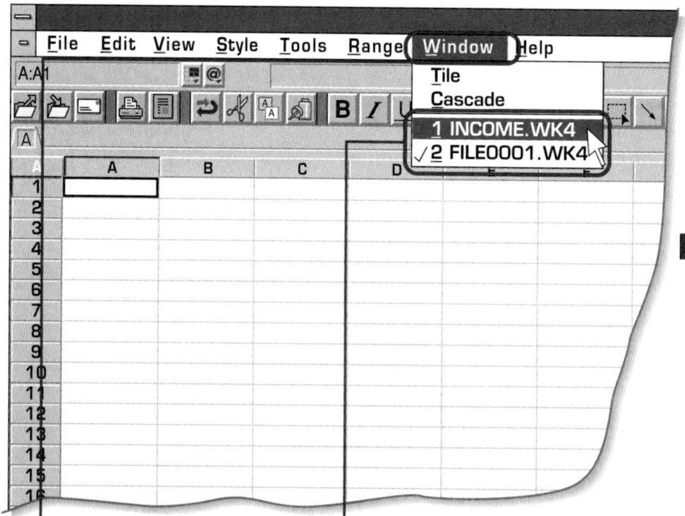

1 Move the mouse over **Window** and then press the left button.

◆ A list of all your open files appears. The current file displays a check mark (✓) beside its name.

2 Move the mouse over the file you want to view and then press the left button.

You can easily switch between all of your open files. This lets you view the contents of each file.

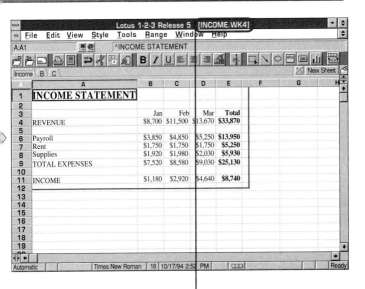

◆ The file appears.

◆ The name of the file appears at the top of your screen.

211

CLOSE A FILE

CLOSE A FILE

Close the active window

| File | Edit | View | Style | Tools | Range | Window | Help |

| A: | | | NCOME STATEMENT |

New

Open... Ctrl+O

Close

Save Ctrl+S

Save As...

Doc Info...

Protect...

Send Mail...

Print Preview...

Page Setup...

Print... Ctrl+P

Printer Setup...

Exit

1 INCOME.WK4

| | B | I | U |

| | B | C | D | E |

NT

	Jan	Feb	Mar	Total
	$8,700	$11,500	$13,670	$33,87
	$3,850	$4,850	$5,250	$13,9
	$1,750	$1,750	$1,750	$5
	$1,920	$1,980	$2,030	$3
	$7,520	$8,580	$9,030	$2
	$1,180	$2,920	$4,640	

1 To save the file before closing, refer to page 50.

2 Move the mouse over **File** and then press the left button.

3 Move the mouse over **Close** and then press the left button.

212

When you finish working with a file, you can close the file to remove it from your screen.

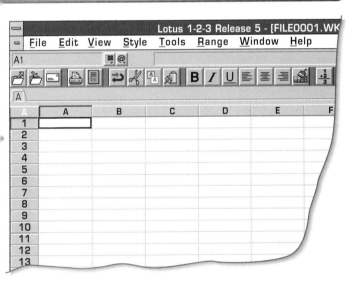

◆ The file disappears from your screen.

CREATE A CHART

CREATE A CHART

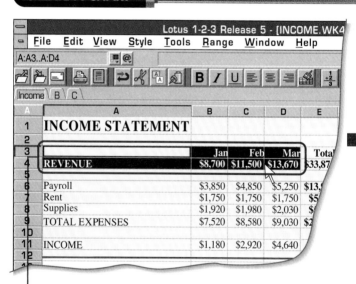

1 Select the cells containing the data you want to chart, including the row and column titles.

Note: To select cells, refer to pages 26 to 29.

You can create a chart directly from your worksheet data.

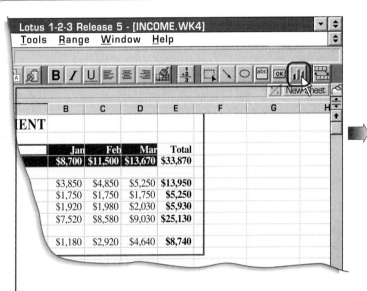

Lotus 1-2-3 Release 5 - [INCOME.WK4]

Tools   Range   Window   Help

	B	C	D	E	F	G	H
ENT							
	Jan	**Feb**	**Mar**	**Total**			
	$8,700	**$11,500**	**$13,670**	**$33,870**			
	$3,850	$4,850	$5,250	**$13,950**			
	$1,750	$1,750	$1,750	**$5,250**			
	$1,920	$1,980	$2,030	**$5,930**			
	$7,520	$8,580	$9,030	**$25,130**			
	$1,180	$2,920	$4,640	**$8,740**			

2 Move the mouse ⬉ over 📊 and then press the left button.

To continue, refer to the next page.

215

CREATE A CHART

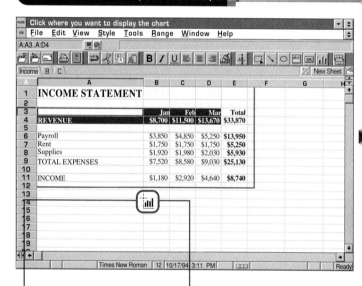

3 Move the mouse ⌖ over your worksheet and ⌖ changes to ⓘⓘⓘ.

4 Move the mouse ⓘⓘⓘ over the location where you want the top left corner of the chart to appear and then press the left button.

216

If you make changes to data in your worksheet, 1-2-3 will automatically update the chart to reflect the changes.

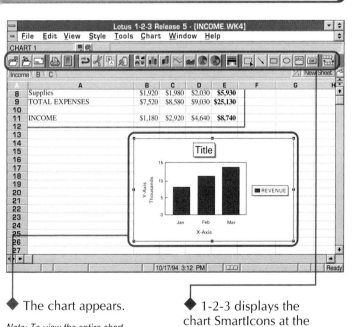

◆ The chart appears.

Note: To view the entire chart, use the scroll bar. For more information, refer to page 40.

◆ 1-2-3 displays the chart SmartIcons at the top of your screen.

217

MOVE A CHART

MOVE A CHART

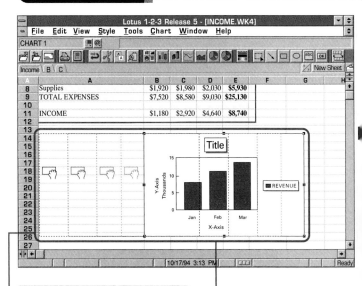

1 To move a chart, move the mouse ⌖ over an edge of the chart (not a handle ■).

2 Press and hold down the left button as you drag the chart to a new location.

◆ A dotted box indicates the new location.

After you
create a chart, you
can move it to a more
suitable location in
your worksheet.

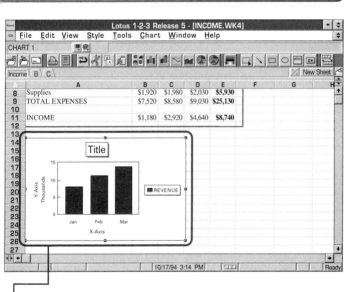

3 Release the button
and the chart moves to
the new location.

219

SIZE A CHART

You can change the size of a chart using any handle around the chart.

SIZE A CHART

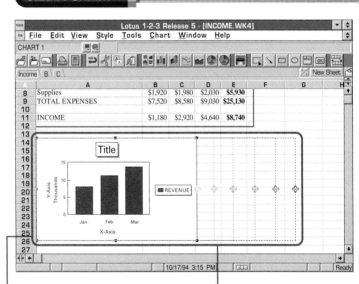

1 Move the mouse ↖ over an edge of the chart and then press the left button. Handles (■) appear around the chart.

2 Move the mouse ↖ over one of the handles (■) and ↖ changes to ✥.

3 Press and hold down the left button as you drag the chart to a new size.

◆ A dotted box indicates the new size.

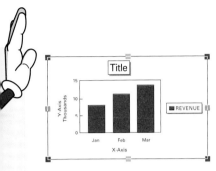

■ You can use these handles to change the height of a chart.

■ You can use these handles to change the width of a chart.

■ You can use these handles to change the height and width of a chart at the same time.

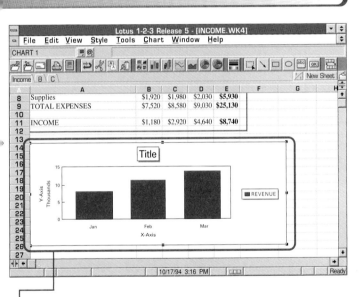

4 Release the button and the chart displays the new size.

CHANGE CHART TITLES

CHANGE CHART TITLES

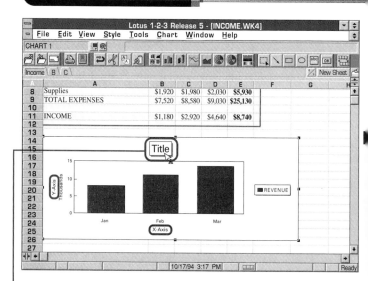

1 Move the mouse ⬚ over the title you want to change and then quickly press the left button twice.

◆ A dialog box appears.

*Note: The dialog box that appears depends on the title you selected in step **1**.*

You can change the titles in your chart to make the chart more meaningful.

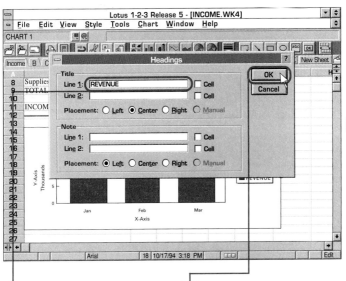

2 Type the new title (example: **REVENUE**).

3 Move the mouse ⌖ over **OK** and then press the left button.

To continue, refer to the next page.

CHANGE CHART TITLES

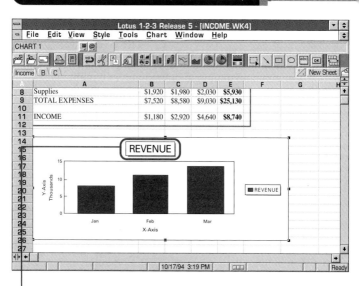

◆ The chart displays the new title.

Note: To deselect the title, move the mouse ⛶ outside the title area and then press the left button.

Chart titles help to clearly define the information displayed in your chart.

DELETE CHART TITLES

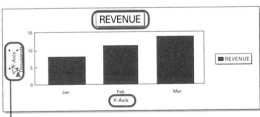

1 Move the mouse over the title you want to delete (example: **Y-Axis**) and then press the left button. Handles (■) appear around the title.

2 Press Delete on your keyboard.

CHANGE CHART TYPE

CHANGE CHART TYPE

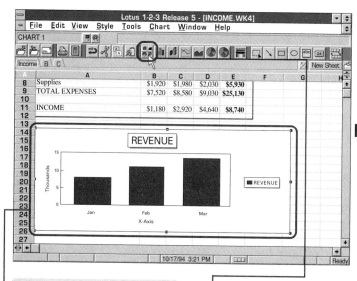

1 To select the chart you want to change, move the mouse ⟍ over the chart and then press the left button.

2 Move the mouse ⟍ over 🔲 and then press the left button.

After creating
a chart, you can
select a new chart type
that will better suit
your data.

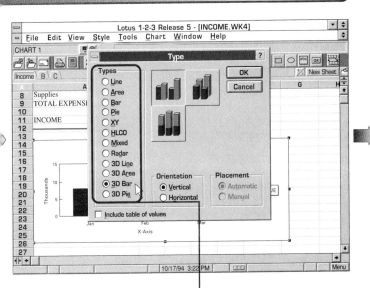

◆ The **Type** dialog box
appears.

3 Move the mouse ⤢ over
the chart type you want to
use (example: **3D Bar**) and
then press the left button.
○ changes to ◉.

To continue, refer to the next page.

227

CHANGE CHART TYPE

CHANGE CHART TYPE (CONTINUED)

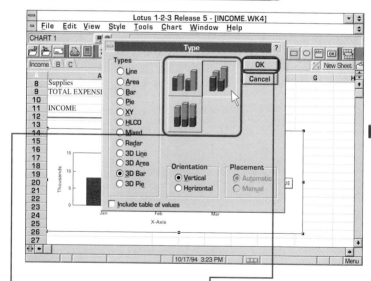

◆ The styles for the chart type you selected appear.

4 Move the mouse ⬚ over the style you want to use and then press the left button.

5 Move the mouse ⬚ over **OK** and then press the left button.

1-2-3 offers a variety of styles for each chart type.

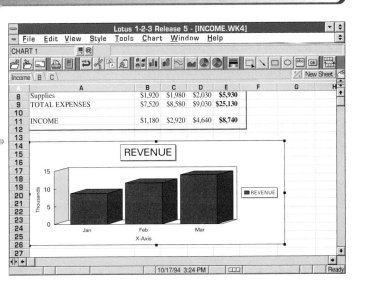

◆ The new chart type appears.

229

PRINT A CHART

PRINT A CHART ON ITS OWN PAGE

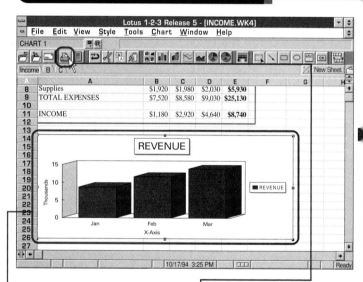

1 To print a chart on its own page, move the mouse ⬁ over the chart and then press the left button.

2 Move the mouse ⬁ over 🖨 and then press the left button.

> You can
> print your chart on
> its own page without
> the worksheet
> data.

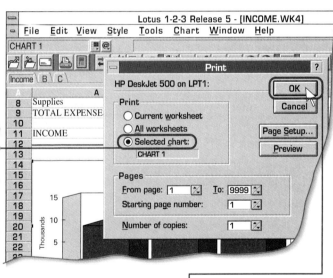

◆ The **Print** dialog box appears.

3 Move the mouse ⍦ over **Selected chart:** and then press the left button (○ changes to ◉).

4 Move the mouse ⍦ over **OK** and then press the left button.

PRINT A CHART

PRINT A CHART WITH THE WORKSHEET DATA

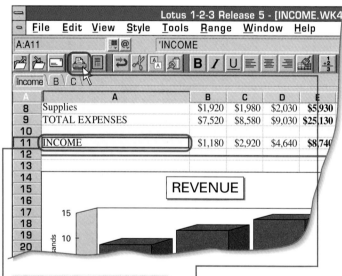

Lotus 1-2-3 Release 5 - [INCOME.WK4]

File   Edit   View   Style   Tools   Range   Window   Help

A:A11   ▣ @   'INCOME

Income │ B │ C

A	A	B	C	D	E
8	Supplies	$1,920	$1,980	$2,030	$5,930
9	TOTAL EXPENSES	$7,520	$8,580	$9,030	$25,130
10					
11	INCOME	$1,180	$2,920	$4,640	$8,740
12					
13					

REVENUE

1 To print a chart with the worksheet data, move the mouse ⇗ over any cell in the worksheet and then press the left button.

2 Move the mouse ⇗ over 🖨 and then press the left button.

You can print your chart with the worksheet data.

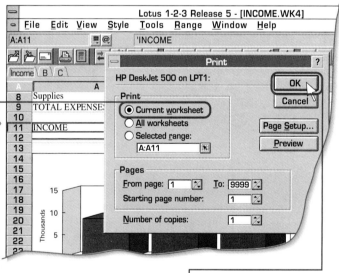

◆ The **Print** dialog box appears.

3 Move the mouse ⌖ over **Current worksheet:** and then press the left button (O changes to ◉).

4 Move the mouse ⌖ over **OK** and then press the left button.

233

CREATE A MAP

USA by State

CREATE A MAP

1-2-3 will automatically create a map that corresponds to the regions you enter in your worksheet. 1-2-3 provides maps for the following locations:

Alaska
Australia by State
Canada by Province
Europe by Country
European Union by Region
Hawaii

Japan by Prefecture
Mexico by Estado
Taiwan
USA by State
World Countries

You can use the Map feature to connect your worksheet data to a geographic map.

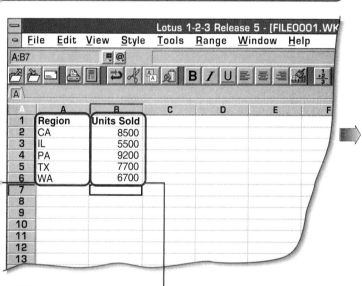

Lotus 1-2-3 Release 5 - [FILE0001.WK

File Edit View Style Tools Range Window Help

A:B7

	A	B	C	D	E	F
1	Region	Units Sold				
2	CA	8500				
3	IL	5500				
4	PA	9200				
5	TX	7700				
6	WA	6700				
7						
8						
9						
10						
11						
12						
13						

1 Enter the names of the regions or map codes (example: **Texas** or **TX**) in one column.

Note: This example adds a map to a new file. To create a new file, refer to page 206.

2 Enter the data for each region in the next column.

To continue, refer to the next page.

235

CREATE A MAP

USA by State

CREATE A MAP (CONTINUED)

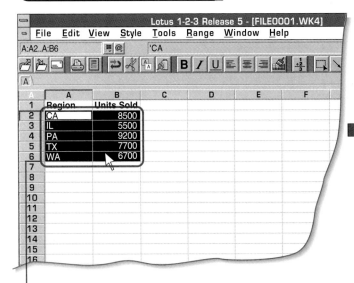

Lotus 1-2-3 Release 5 - [FILE0001.WK4]

File   Edit   View   Style   Tools   Range   Window   Help

A:A2..A:B6   'CA

	A	B	C	D	E	F
1	Region	Units Sold				
2	CA	8500				
3	IL	5500				
4	PA	9200				
5	TX	7700				
6	WA	6700				
7						
8						
9						
10						
11						
12						
13						
14						
15						
16						

3 Select the cells containing the data you want to map.

Note: To select cells, refer to pages 26 to 29.

> Creating
> a map is useful when
> you want to display
> sales information
> by region.

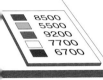

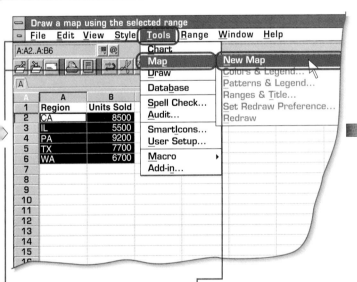

Draw a map using the selected range

File   Edit   View   Style   **Tools**   Range   Window   Help

A:A2..A:B6

Chart
Map ▶   **New Map**
Draw   Colors & Legend...
Database   Patterns & Legend...
Spell Check...   Ranges & Title...
Audit...   Set Redraw Preference...
SmartIcons...   Redraw
User Setup...
Macro ▶
Add-in...

	A	B
1	Region	Units Sold
2	CA	8500
3	IL	5500
4	PA	9200
5	TX	7700
6	WA	6700
7		
8		
9		
10		
11		
12		
13		
14		
15		

4 Move the mouse ▷ over **Tools** and then press the left button.

5 Move the mouse ▷ over **Map** and then press the left button.

6 Move the mouse ▷ over **New Map** and then press the left button.

To continue, refer to the next page.

237

CREATE A MAP

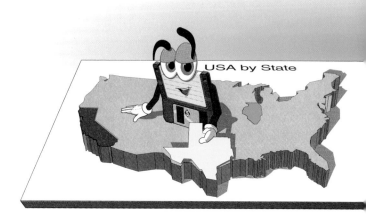

USA by State

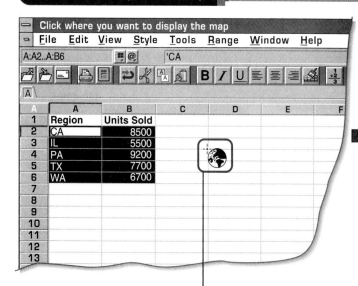

Click where you want to display the map

| | File | Edit | View | Style | Tools | Range | Window | Help |

A:A2..A:B6   'CA

B *I* U

	A	B	C	D	E	F
1	**Region**	**Units Sold**				
2	CA	8500				
3	IL	5500				
4	PA	9200				
5	TX	7700				
6	WA	6700				
7						
8						
9						
10						
11						
12						
13						

7 Move the mouse ⃠ over your worksheet and ⃠ changes to 🌐.

8 Move the mouse 🌐 over the location where you want the top left corner of the map to appear and then press the left button.

238

> If you make changes to data in your worksheet, 1-2-3 will automatically update the map to reflect the changes.

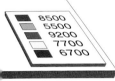

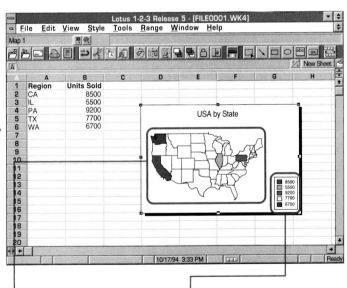

◆ A map appears, highlighting the regions from your worksheet in various colors.

◆ The map divides the regions into groups and assigns a color to each group.

INDEX

Lotus 1-2-3

Exit, 58-59
Introduction, 2-5
Start, 10-13

A

Absolute
  References, 114-117
Add Numbers, 106-107
Align Data, 140-141
Appearance, Numbers,
  Change, 134-135
Automatic
  Recalculation, 94-95

B

Bold Data, 138-139
Borders, Add, 156-161
Break, Page, 174-177

C

Cells
  Current, 16-17
  Definition, 15
  Select, 26-29

Center Data Across
  Columns, 152-155
Change, Undo Last, 72-73
Charts
  Create, 214-217
  Move, 218-219
  Print, 230-233
  Size, 220-221
  Titles, Change, 222-225
  Type, Change, 226-229
Check Spelling, 82-87
Close File, 212-213
Columns
  Definition, 15
  Delete, 124-125
  Insert, 120-121
  Select, 27
  Width, Change, 126-129
Commands, Select, 30-37
Copy
  Data, 78-81, 202-205
  Formulas, 110-117
Create
  Chart, 214-217
  File, 206-209
  Map, 234-239

D

Data
  Align, 140-141
  Bold, 138-139
  Center Across
    Columns, 152-155
  Copy, 78-81
  Copy/Move Between
    Worksheets, 202-205
  Delete, 70-71

Edit, 66-69
Enter, 18-21
Enter Automatically, 22-25
Font Size,
  Change, 144-145
Fonts, Change, 146-151
Italicize, 138-139
Move, 74-77
Printed Size,
  Change, 184-187
Style
  Automatically, 162-165
Typeface,
  Change, 142-143
Underline, 138-139
Decimal Places,
  Change, 136-137
Delete
  Columns, 124-125
  Data, 70-71
  Rows, 122-123
Directories, 48-49
Drives, 46-47

E

Edit Data, 66-69
Enter
  Data, 18-25
  Formulas, 92-93
  Functions, 100-105
Errors, Formulas, 108-109
Exit Lotus 1-2-3, 58-59

F

Files
  Close, 212-213
  Create, 206-209
  Open, 60-65
  Save, 50-53
  Save To Diskette, 54-57
  Switch Between, 210-211
Floppy Drives, 47
Font Size, Change, 144-145
Fonts, Change, 146-151
Formulas
  Copy, 110-117
  Enter, 92-93
  Errors, 108-109
  Introduction, 88-91
Functions
  Enter, 100-105
  Introduction, 96-99

H

Hard Drives, 47, 49
Help, 42-45

INDEX

I

Insert
  Columns, 120-121
  Rows, 118-119
  Worksheet, 192-193
Italicize Data, 138-139

J

Justify Data, 140-141

M

Magnify Page, 170-171
Map, Create, 234-239
Margins, Change, 180-183
Menus, Using, 30-33
Mouse
  Parts, 8-9
  Terms, 8-9
  Using, 6-9
Move
  Chart, 218-219
  Data, 74-77, 202-205
  Through Worksheet, 38-41

N

Name Worksheet, 196-197
Numbers
  Add, 106-107
  Appearance,
    Change, 134-135
  Decimal Places,
    Change, 136-137

O

Open Files, 60-65
Operators, 88
Orientation, Page,
  Change, 178-179

P

Page
  Break, 174-177
  Magnify, 170-171
  Margins, Change, 180-183
  Orientation,
    Change, 178-179
Preview
  Worksheet, 166-171
Print
  Chart, 230-233
  Worksheet, 172-173
Printed Data Size,
  Change, 184-187

Q

Quick Menus, Using, 36-37

R

Recalculation,
  Automatic, 94-95
References,
  Relative/Absolute, 110-117
Relative
  References, 110-113
Rows
  Definition, 15
  Delete, 122-123
  Height, Change, 130-133
  Insert, 118-119
  Select, 26

S

Save File, 50-53
Save File To Diskette, 54-57
Scroll, 40-41
Select
  Cells, 26-29
  Commands, 30-37
Size
  Chart, Change, 220-221
  Printed Data,
    Change, 184-187
SmartIcons
  Display Different, 190-191
  Using, 34-35
Spelling, Check, 82-87
Start Lotus 1-2-3, 10-13
Style Data
  Automatically, 162-165
Switch Between
  Files, 210-211
Switch Between
  Worksheets, 194-195

T

Titles, Chart,
  Change, 222-225
Type, Chart,
  Change, 226-229
Typeface, Change, 142-143

U

Underline Data, 138-139
Undo Last Change, 72-73

V

View Multiple
  Worksheets, 198-201
View One Worksheet, 201

W

Worksheets
  Basics, 14-15
  Copy Data
    Between, 202-205
  Insert, 192-193
  Move Data
    Between, 202-205
  Move Through, 38-41
  Name, 196-197
  Preview, 166-171
  Print, 172-173
  Switch Between, 194-195
  View Multiple, 198-201
  View One, 201

Z

Zoom In/Out, 188-189

ORDER FORM

TRADE & INDIVIDUAL ORDERS

Phone: **(800) 762-2974**
or **(317) 895-5200**
(8 a.m.–6 p.m., CST, weekdays)
FAX : **(317) 895-5298**

CORPORATE ORDERS FOR INTROGRAPHIC BOOKS

Phone: **(800) 469-6616** *ext.* **206**
(8 a.m.–5 p.m., EST, weekdays)
FAX : **(905) 890-9434**

Qty	ISBN	Title	Price	Total

Shipping & Handling Charges

	Description	First book	Each add'l. book	Total
Domestic	Normal	$4.50	$1.50	$
	Two Day Air	$8.50	$2.50	$
	Overnight	$18.00	$3.00	$
International	Surface	$8.00	$8.00	$
	Airmail	$16.00	$16.00	$
	DHL Air	$17.00	$17.00	$

Subtotal _____

CA residents add
applicable sales tax _____

IN, MA and MD
residents add
5% sales tax _____

IL residents add
6.25% sales tax _____

RI residents add
7% sales tax _____

TX residents add
8.25% sales tax _____

Shipping _____

Total _____

Ship to:

Name _____

Address_____

Company _____

City/State/Zip _____

Daytime Phone_____

Payment: □ Check to IDG Books (US Funds Only)
  □ Visa □ Mastercard □ American Express

Card # _____ Exp. _____

Signature_____

IDG Books Education Group
Jim Kelly, Director of Education Sales – 9 Village Circle, Ste. 450, Westlake, TX 76262
800-434-2086 Phone • 817-430-5852 Fax • 8:30-5:00 CST

IDG BOOKS WORLDWIDE REGISTRATION CARD

IDG BOOKS

THE WORLD OF
COMPUTER
KNOWLEDGE

Title of this book: LOTUS 1-2-3 R5 FOR WINDOWS VISUAL POCKET GUIDE

My overall rating of this book:
❑ Very good [1] ❑ Good [2] ❑ Satisfactory [3] ❑ Fair [4] ❑ Poor [5]

How I first heard about this book:
❑ Found in bookstore; name: [6]

❑ Book review: [7]

❑ Advertisement: [8]

❑ Catalog: [9]

❑ Word of mouth; heard about book from friend, co-worker, etc.: [10]

❑ Other: [11]

What I liked most about this book:

What I would change, add, delete, etc., in future editions of this book:

Other comments:

Number of computer books I purchase in a year: ❑ 1 [12] ❑ 2-5 [13] ❑ 6-10 [14] ❑ More than 10 [15]

I would characterize my computer skills as:
❑ Beginner [16] ❑ Intermediate [17] ❑ Advanced [18] ❑ Professional [19]

I use ❑ DOS [20] ❑ Windows [21] ❑ OS/2 [22] ❑ Unix [23] ❑ Macintosh [24] ❑ Other: [25]_____
(please specify)

I would be interested in new books on the following subjects:
(please check all that apply, and use the spaces provided to identify specific software)

❑ Word processing: [26]   ❑ Spreadsheets: [27]

❑ Data bases: [28]   ❑ Desktop publishing: [29]

❑ File Utilities: [30]   ❑ Money management: [31]

❑ Networking: [32]   ❑ Programming languages: [33]

❑ Other: [34]

I use a PC at (please check all that apply): ❑ home [35] ❑ work [36] ❑ school [37] ❑ other: [38] _____

The disks I prefer to use are ❑ 5.25 [39] ❑ 3.5 [40] ❑ other: [41]_____

I have a CD ROM: ❑ yes [42]   ❑ no [43]

I plan to buy or upgrade computer hardware this year: ❑ yes [44] ❑ no [45]

I plan to buy or upgrade computer software this year: ❑ yes [46] ❑ no [47]

Name: _____ Business title: [48] _____

Type of Business: [49]

Address (❑ home [50] ❑ work [51]/Company name: _____)

Street/Suite#

City [52]/State [53]/Zipcode [54]: _____ Country [55]

❑ **I liked this book!**
You may quote me by name in future IDG Books Worldwide promotional materials.

My daytime phone number is _____

☐ YES!
Please keep me informed about IDG's World of Computer Knowledge. Send me the latest IDG Books catalog.

NO POSTAGE
NECESSARY
IF MAILED
IN THE
UNITED STATES

BUSINESS REPLY MAIL
FIRST CLASS MAIL   PERMIT NO. 2605   SAN MATEO, CALIFORNIA

IDG Books Worldwide
155 Bovet Rd
San Mateo CA 94402-9833